Growing Up with Technology

Growing Up with Technology explores the role of technology in the everyday lives of three- and four-year-old children, presenting the implications for children's continuing learning and development.

Children are growing up in a world where the internet, mobile phones and other forms of digital interaction are features of daily life. The authors have carefully observed children's experiences at home and analysed the perspectives of parents, practitioners and the children themselves. This has enabled them to provide a nuanced account of the different ways in which technology can support or inhibit learning.

Drawing on evidence from their research, the authors bring a fresh approach to these debates, based on establishing relationships with children, families and educators to get insights into practices, values and attitudes.

A number of key questions are considered, including:

- Which technologies do young children encounter at home and preschool?
- What kind of learning takes place in these encounters?
- How can parents and practitioners support this learning?
- Are some children disadvantaged when it comes to learning with technology?

Growing Up with Technology is strongly grounded in a series of research projects, providing new ways of thinking about how children's learning with technology can be supported. It will be of great interest to undergraduate and postgraduate students on a range of courses, including childhood studies, and those with a particular interest in the use of technology in education. Parents, practitioners and researchers will also find this a fascinating and informative read.

Lydia Plowman is Professor of Education and **Christine Stephen** is Research Fellow, both at the Stirling Institute of Education, University of Stirling. **Joanna McPake** is Reader, Faculty of Education, University of Strathclyde.

Growing Up with Technology

Young children learning in a digital world

Lydia Plowman, Christine Stephen
and Joanna McPake

Routledge
Taylor & Francis Group

LONDON AND NEW YORK

First published 2010
by Routledge
2 Park Square, Milton Park, Abingdon, Oxon OX14 4RN

Simultaneously published in the USA and Canada
by Routledge
270 Madison Avenue, New York, NY 10016

Routledge is an imprint of the Taylor & Francis Group, an informa business

© 2010 Lydia Plowman, Christine Stephen and Joanna McPake

Typeset in Bembo and Gill
by Keystroke, Tettenhall, Wolverhampton
Printed and bound in Great Britain
by TJ International Ltd, Padstow, Cornwall

British Library Cataloguing in Publication Data
A catalogue record for this book is available from the British Library

Library of Congress Cataloging-in-Publication Data
Plowman, Lydia.
   Growing up with technology : young children learning in a digital world / Lydia Plowman,
Christine Stephen and Joanna McPake.
      p. cm.
   1. Technology and children. 2. Internet and children. 3. Digital media. 4. Mass media and
children. 5. Digital electronics. I. Stephen, Christine. II. McPake, Joanna. III. Title.
   HQ784.T37P56 2010
   302.23'1083—dc22   2009025279

ISBN 10: 0–415–46891–4 (hbk)
ISBN 10: 0–415–46892–2 (pbk)
ISBN 10: 0–203–86361–5 (ebk)

ISBN 13: 978–0–415–46891–6 (hbk)
ISBN 13: 978–0–415–46892–3 (pbk)
ISBN 13: 978–0–203–86361–9 (ebk)

Contents

Figures

Tables

Tables

Acknowledgements

We are indebted to the children, families and education professionals who participated in the studies described in this book. They welcomed us into their homes and workplaces, were generous with their time and made our involvement in this research endlessly fascinating and enjoyable.

We had the good fortune to work with fantastic researchers as part of the project teams: Claire Adey, Sarah Berch-Heyman, Susi Downey, Konstantina Martzoukou, Daniela Sime and Olivia Stevenson. We appreciate the energy, patience, hard work and good humour that they contributed.

The research reported in this book is based on three projects funded by the Economic and Social Research Council: 'Young children learning with toys and technology at home' (RES–062–23–0507), 'Entering e-Society: Young children's development of e-literacy' (RES–341–25–0034) and 'Interplay: Play, Learning and ICT in Pre-school Education' (RES–139–25–0006). 'Already at a Disadvantage? Children's access to ICT at home and their preparation for primary school' was funded by Becta and a series of small-scale projects were funded by Learning and Teaching Scotland. We are grateful for this support.

Permission has been granted by Taylor & Francis to reproduce Figures 5.3 and 5.4 and Table 8.1 and from John Wiley to reproduce Tables 5.1 and 5.2.

Acknowledgements

Introduction

Evie and Andy

Evie, age four

Evie MacGregor is sitting on the floor with her pink LeapPad bag. She opens the bag, takes out three books and then takes out the LeapPad itself. She opens the LeapPad – an interactive storybook console – places it on the floor and inserts a book of princess stories. 'I like the princess one. I like playing Cinderella,' she says. 'I'll turn the page to my favourite bit.' She tries to fit the cartridge into the slot but it is the wrong way round. So she flips it and then turns the LeapPad on. She points with the magic pen at pictures on the pages so that the LeapPad speaks. Touching pictures on the page, she listens to the instructions in order to play a game. She then uses the pen to indicate the correct answers to questions the LeapPad asks. The questions involve identifying colours and characters from the story. She is proud of how fast she can do this: 'I'm faster than my Mum,' she tells the researcher. She does these activities without any help from her parents. 'She's good at sussing things out. The more it makes her think, the better she is at it,' Mrs MacGregor comments. Evie agrees that she learnt to use it by herself: 'I figured it out.'

Evie is four years old and lives with her parents in a village in central Scotland. Their home is one of several in a development built early in the twentieth century for workers on the estate of a local landowner. The development is now run as social housing. Her parents were brought up in the nearby town and feel lucky to have been able to secure a house in the village, where Evie has the chance to grow up in a safe, rural environment.

Her parents do not regard themselves as very technologically minded. Mr MacGregor has not needed to learn to use computers or other techno-logical items for the jobs he has had since he left school. He was first a meat packer and currently works as a driver. Mrs MacGregor took a college course in office skills as a teenager and learnt to use some basic word-processing and spreadsheet packages. However, she never had a job where she could use these skills and thinks they must be out of date by now. They bought a computer about a year ago, mainly for Mrs MacGregor to use for household purposes. She uses it to type letters and has not learnt to use all of the equipment, such as the scanner, which came with it. 'I'm not really sure why we bought it now,' she comments. They do not have an internet connection as they are confused by the various packages on offer.

Evie is not allowed to use the computer because it was expensive and she might damage it. Instead, they bought her a toy laptop when she was three years old, but she outgrew it. For Christmas they bought her a LeapPad, which is currently her favourite toy. She can spend up to an hour a day playing with it, usually before bedtime. However, the MacGregors are not particularly concerned about whether or not Evie learns to use technological items such as computers before she starts school. On the basis of their own experience, they think technology is overrated. They prefer Evie to spend time on more traditional activities, such as playing outside and painting and drawing indoors: 'She's never happier than when she's covered in muck or paint.' She has a slide in her back garden and looks after two guinea pigs, which she keeps there. Sometimes, she goes round to the school playground where they have a rope bridge and where she can ride her bike or chalk out a hopscotch game on the tarmac.

Mrs MacGregor also worries that spending too much time on technological activities could be damaging to young children's health: 'You see kids plonked in front of the TV, with no encouragement to run about, and then they put on weight. I'm not sure if some of the violence from computer games doesn't spill over into everyday life. I don't know if this is actually the reason for violence but I think it's damaging if children watch TV or play video games all day long.'

Evie goes to nursery in the nearby town and has been attending full time since the age of two. It does not have much in the way of technology. There is a computer on which Evie sometimes does colouring, but she prefers traditional painting and drawing. Her favourite activity at nursery is playing outside with the other children. She has recently learnt to write her name and to spell some simple words. She will be starting primary school in the village after the summer. It is a very small school, with 18 pupils altogether, but there are ten computers. However, Mr and Mrs MacGregor suppose that these are largely used by the older children. They think Evie might be allowed to look at things on the computer, but not do any work on them.

Andy, age four

Andy Kerr pushes buttons enthusiastically on his Game Boy while explaining to researchers how the game he is playing works. It is a game where you match shapes and try to get rid of pairs as fast as possible from the screen to uncover another scene underneath. 'You have to get two the same so that they go away so I just have to do the rest. You get all of them out of the way and then you can see what Franklin's doing! You press these arrows to get different things, so you press that and then . . . that means I win!' 'How did you know which buttons to press?' asks a researcher. 'Because all the other games do it. It's just the same, but different characters.'

Andy is a four-year-old boy living with his parents and his two-year-old brother, Daniel, in a new housing estate on the outskirts of a town in central Scotland. He is a sociable and articulate boy, keen to show the researchers his favourite toys, which include a battery-operated toy chainsaw, a Woody doll (a character from *Toy Story*), a teddy bear and a *Star Wars* light sabre. He also has some electronic toys which are not working because the batteries are run down. Mrs Kerr describes him as a boy who always wants his toys to do something. When he was little, he thought that teddy bears and other soft toys were 'broken' because they did not respond to poking or pressing.

The family has a computer with broadband internet connection which Andy is allowed to play on while Daniel is asleep – otherwise Daniel tries to join in but just presses keys at random. This means that he can play for between 30 minutes and one hour at a time. If Daniel wakes up, he saves the game and goes back to it later. He has been using the computer for about a year, and has a number of games on CD-ROMs: *Dora the Explorer*, *Putt Putt*, *Twitties*, *Winnie the Pooh* and *Barney*. He also plays games from the CBeebies and Nick Jr. websites, some of which he can play on his own and some of which he plays with help from his dad. At weekends, Andy and his dad surf the web, usually looking for sites his dad thinks will be of interest. These can be sites connected to television programmes Andy has been watching or books he has been reading. Sometimes Andy memorizes web addresses he has seen on advertisements on television and they look them up together.

Andy learnt to play on the Game Boy and the PlayStation at the home of his nine-year-old cousin. He was given his own Game Boy as a Christmas present and he plays it regularly, for 20 to 30 minutes at a time, but not every day. He plays on his own and very rarely asks his parents for help; he only needs help when he has a new game and he needs his parents to read the instructions to him.

Andy also likes football and swimming. He has been having swimming lessons for a year and has certificates commemorating his achievements. He likes playing in the back garden, on the climbing frame and on his bike in the courtyard area that is shared by four houses on the estate. Two of his friends from nursery live in other houses facing the courtyard, and they play on their bikes together.

Mr Kerr is an IT consultant and Mrs Kerr works part time as a social worker. The home computer was bought so that Mr Kerr could do some of his work from home. He also uses it for domestic purposes, such as booking holiday flights, banking and storing digital photographs. Mrs Kerr describes herself as 'really bad with computers'. She has occasionally used the computer to send emails, but knows that she is going to have to become more competent as aspects of her work now require staff to be computer literate. She sees Andy as more accomplished than she is, and recognizes that it is important for him to learn to use technologies while he is young as he will need to use them when he is an adult.

Andy has been attending nursery part time for 18 months. He likes playing with construction toys and dressing up, but he is not very keen on art and craft activities. The nursery has a computer but Andy has not shown much interest in it. The games are more basic than those he plays at home. At nursery he has learnt the alphabet and has been using 'getting ready to read' books.

After the summer he will go to a primary school in town. The nursery children make a series of visits to the school and the playground to meet some of the ten-year-old pupils who will become their 'buddies' when they start school. There will be three computers in his classroom. Andy sees the main incentive for going to school as learning to read, so that he can read the instructions on computer games.

Young children and technology

Growing Up with Technology explores the role of technology in the everyday lives of young children in the UK by describing and examining their experiences at home and in preschool settings. Children such as Evie and Andy are growing up in a world where the internet, mobile phones and various forms of digital interaction are features of daily life. We describe how factors such as their own preferences, the people in their lives, the cultural practices of different environments and the availability of material resources shape their encounters with technology. We focus on children's learning, drawing on a sequence of research projects to examine the ways in which technology can support or hinder learning in the different arenas of home and preschool.

Many people believe that children need to become competent users of digital technologies to avoid disadvantages or marginalization and to become assured, discriminating and effective members of society. However, the ubiquity of these technologies has led to public debate about the ways in which they are seen to exert influence in the lives of young children. We draw on evidence from our research to bring a fresh approach to these debates. This approach is based on establishing relationships with children, families and educators to get insights into practices, values and attitudes. We believe that it is worthwhile to give an account of these research studies because there are choices to be made about the role of technologies in children's lives. *Growing Up with Technology* provides a rich description of children's experiences with technology which can be used to inform these choices.

Chapter 1

Growing up with technology

The children in our studies were three or four years old. Like Evie and Andy, they used technologies in different ways. They went to nursery, enjoyed active lives and engaged in a diverse range of pursuits with friends and family. While all the children had exposure to technologies at home, their experiences varied: some children lived in homes with high levels of technology, but preferred to read books, draw pictures or play with toys; other children lived in homes where parents lacked confidence or interest in how to use technology, yet the children were able to find creative ways of integrating technology into their play. Evie's favourite toy was the LeapPad but, apart from that, she did not show much interest in technology, preferring to look after her guinea pigs, play hopscotch or draw pictures. Andy was a keen Game Boy player and enjoyed surfing the web with his dad, but he also liked dressing up, playing football and swimming.

Where families were enthusiastic users of technology, parents encouraged their children's engagement with computer games or websites such as CBeebies and Nick Jr. In these families, children's developing competences with technology were noted with pride and seen as necessary for a successful future. Andy's mother believed this, too. Unlike her husband, she was no enthusiast but reluctantly acknowledged that she would need to familiarize herself with computers for her own career. There was no need for technology in the MacGregors' working lives and, in any case, they did not have much in the way of spare income to buy products and they were worried about the effect they might have on Evie's play. Other parents said that they were not against digital technologies, but they would leave introducing them until their child indicated interest, preferring to encourage imaginative games with dolls or outdoor play. Most of the parents had some ambivalence about the ways in which technology could be beneficial or detrimental to their children's well-being and described uncertainty about the role it should play in their family, sometimes expressing contradictory views within the same interview.

Although the vignettes of Evie and Andy may reinforce some stereotypes – Evie is a girl, is not very interested in technology and is from a financially-disadvantaged home and Andy is a boy, likes technology and is from a financially-advantaged home – overall these different patterns of experience and attitude were not divided by the socioeconomic status of the families. We found a more complex picture in which there was often a stronger link between parents' own experiences of technology in the workplace or in educational settings and the ways in which these experiences influenced the opportunities they offered their children. Although some children had more access to technology at nursery than they did at home, we found very different patterns of provision and support there, too. In circumstances such as these, in which children are exposed to a wide range of experiences before they start school, do we need to be concerned that some children are disadvantaged compared to others in terms of their opportunities to use technologies? If so, what does this mean for their future education? These questions are of more than academic interest when governments increasingly see education as an opportunity to familiarize young children with the technologies associated with global knowledge economies.

Preparing children for the knowledge economy

UK governments see computers as having the potential to improve the standards of pupils' school education, and they have invested accordingly. Since the 1980s, when the BBC microcomputer was introduced, through to the National Grid for Learning in the 1990s and the Home Access scheme, which launched in England in 2009, children are seen as needing to be prepared for working in the knowledge economy – a metaphor which implicitly associates brain work with technology and its economic benefits. There has been heavy investment in the Home Access scheme to promote the educational benefits of home computer and internet access (Becta 2008) as part of the strategy to ease the transition to a knowledge-based economy. As it will be 15 years until most three- and four-year-olds enter the labour market, policy interest has not focused on technology for this age group until comparatively recently. Interest surfaced around the turn of the millennium and is driven by a desire to prepare children of all ages for what is seen as an increasingly complex and technological world. For instance, the *Digital Britain* report, produced by two government departments, states that 'in education and training for digital life skills, we need a step change in approach, starting with the youngest' (BERR/DCMS 2009: 64). It is now widely accepted by policy makers that the pattern for success in later life is established in the preschool years. For example, the *Early Years Framework* refers to the first years of a child's life as laying the foundations of skills for learning, life and work and having a major bearing on wider outcomes, including employment (Scottish Government 2008a: 7). Similar aspirations are found in the *No Child Left Behind* legislation, which was introduced by the government of the United States in 2002. The primary goal of part D, 'Enhancing Education Through Technology', is to improve student attainment through technology, with the additional goal:

to assist every student in crossing the digital divide by ensuring that every student is technologically literate by the time the student finishes the eighth grade, regardless of the student's race, ethnicity, gender, family income, geographic location, or disability.

(U.S. Department of Education 2002: Section 2042)

Developing the early years curriculum with reference to information and communication technology (ICT) has therefore been a fairly recent phenomenon, and the countries of the UK and elsewhere are at different stages of implementation. Research in this area is still limited compared to the enormous amount of literature on ICT in schools. While it is widely accepted that the opportunities and challenges brought by technologies should be addressed for the years of compulsory schooling, especially for older children who will enter employment more imminently, there has, so far, been less attention to the period before children start school. Introducing ICT into preschools is not simply a matter of adapting policies that have been developed for schools or of translating findings from schools-based research because there are fundamental differences between these phases of education, as outlined in Chapters 3 and 4. Compared to the years of compulsory education in schools, preschool settings have a distinct culture in terms of different norms of professional practice with reference to adult-directed teaching, emphasis on learning through play, less prescriptive curriculum and concepts of assessment. The notion of computers having a role in driving up standards, as stated in *No Child Left Behind*, is beginning to emerge, but it does not have the high profile it has in schools.

Over the years that we have been engaged in research about preschool children and technology, we have seen many changes: computers have become more commonplace in the playroom, practitioners' confidence has increased and there has been more political interest in the value of home learning. However, the pace of change has not kept up with the technological changes in society and their influence on how we communicate or spend our leisure time: many nurseries continue to think of ICT as being primarily concerned with desktop computers, it is unusual to find activities involving the internet in the playroom and practitioners still find it a challenge to adapt their pedagogy to include technology. This slow pace of change is highlighted by a recent report published for Becta, an English government agency which promotes the use of technology in learning. The report refers to ICT in schools rather than preschools, and states:

[T]he development of new pedagogies can be a substantial professional challenge: teachers must learn new skills and rethink and refashion the teacher–learner relationship. Developing pedagogical approaches of active learner engagement, facilitating and scaffolding learning rather than transmitting knowledge, using new, more open, questioning techniques, and undertaking assessment for learning all provide significant challenges to a teacher's role and identity. A lack of time, willingness or the resources to develop new pedagogical approaches is a major barrier to fully exploiting the educational potential of digital technology.

(Chowcat, Phillips, Popham and Jones 2008: 20)

This analysis refers to the need for teachers to rethink pedagogy and learn new skills as key challenges for using technology to drive educational change. These are topics that we examine in a preschool context in Chapters 4 and 5. But educational change can be slow. This description of the need for change is being reported more than 20 years after computers were first introduced in schools and in the wake of repeated major capital investments: in his speech to the BETT conference in January 2009, Jim Knight, the Minister for Schools and Learners, announced that more than £5 billion has been spent on ICT for schools in England and Wales over the last decade. Preschool education does not share this history. The urgency to equip playrooms with technology has been mainly absent until the last few years. As an example, the title of our first research report on preschools and ICT is *Come back in two years!* Based on fieldwork carried out in 2002, in the first paragraph we say:

'Come back in two years!' is a quote from a preschool practitioner as she waved goodbye at the end of a research visit to her playgroup. The implied continuation of the sentence was '. . . and then we'll have something to show you'. Like most of our other interviewees, she was enthusiastic about ICTs and had a strong belief in their value, but she was aware that the situation in her playgroup fell short of some undefined notion of 'best practice'. She felt confident that we would see a great transformation if we were to return in two years' time and we often heard comments from other practitioners such as 'it's just a matter of time'.

(Stephen and Plowman 2003a: 2)

Given that attention turned to young children in nurseries long after it was given those aged five to 16 in schools, it is not surprising that changes in preschool pedagogy for integrating ICT are still emerging. In the endnote to the same report we provide the following summary of the analysis we have presented:

Some aspects of this report may, on first reading, seem to present a fairly gloomy scenario of the use of ICT in preschool settings. We report a lack of training, a lack of explicit pedagogy, wide variation in levels of resources and a fairly low level of practitioner skills. However, the underlying tone of this report is optimistic. Practitioners are looking into the future, as our use of the phrase 'Come back in two years!' as the title for this report emphasizes.

Although one of the participants in the study said that positive change was 'just a matter of time', transforming this optimism into practice that will have a positive impact on children has many resource implications. It will require greatly enhanced training opportunities . . . It will also require more guidance in the form of a national strategy for the use of ICT in preschool settings. This will give practitioners the impetus to address the changes in practice that will bring about enhanced learning opportunities for children.

(Stephen and Plowman 2003a: 33)

In drawing attention to pedagogy, resources and training, our commentary echoes the diagnosis on the use of ICT in schools provided by the Becta report mentioned above. Whether in schools or in playrooms, the challenges seem to be enduring. Simply investing in technology or offering training in the mechanics of using equipment will not lead to the sought-after changes; these changes are more likely to be brought about by supporting practitioners across sectors, helping them to feel confident about developing their pedagogy. In the descriptions of our research in the following chapters, we show that there is a role for technology in early years education. However, using it to create learning opportunities depends not only on changes in practice, but also on engaging educators in discussions about the value and desirability of very young children using computers.

The shift in interest to informal education settings is partly the result of a greater appreciation of the kinds of learning and knowledge that can be developed in the home. Typically, this is different from the curricular knowledge found in formal education settings as it is more contingent, more fluid and more grounded in everyday life. As such, it has not been the primary focus of researchers' or education professionals' attention. The recent attempts to make the curriculum less prescriptive and more flexible and responsive build on greater cognizance of the opportunities for learning in the home, particularly in the early years. Having a better understanding of the skills, knowledge and concepts associated with children's experiences at home is central to the ways in which children's learning can be extended in preschool settings; this has been usual practice in the case of literacy and numeracy for a number of years, but children's learning about and with technologies at home has not been valued or even noticed. This means that children's learning on entry to primary school can be focused on operational aspects, such as how to control a mouse or open a file, and does not extend beyond technology for work and study, such as the PC or interactive whiteboard. This book is an attempt to shift the balance in favour of greater understanding of children's everyday activities with a range of technologies at home and to relate this to their experiences at preschool. The aim is not to assist formal education in its colonization of the home, but to enable parents and practitioners to gain a deeper understanding of what children do and can do. We are neither advocates for technology, nor among its detractors. Rather, we describe what we have learnt from our studies and come to some conclusions about the ways in which technology can enhance learning in the right circumstances.

Researching children and technology

From an educational researcher's point of view, the preschool years are a particularly interesting time for investigating children's learning with technology: nurseries and homes offer opportunities to observe the relationship between formal and informal learning, the balance between child-centred and adult-directed activities and the relationship of these technologies to a media environment which encompasses television, DVDs, books and magazines. This book's foundation in empirical research means that its illustrations of practice (through vignettes, extracts from interviews, field notes and photographs) necessarily focus on the technologies that we saw in use. Accordingly, *Growing Up with Technology* is not intended to be a manual for how to introduce technology into preschool settings and it does not present tried and tested activities for practitioners to implement within a particular curriculum. It does not provide a source of advice for parents on what constitutes the right approach to living with technology at home. Rather, we bring insights from a range of perspectives – education, cultural psychology and social studies – to describe and discuss general principles that are likely to be relevant even as the technologies change. Too much focus on the technology would suggest that this book determines practice as well as risk the content becoming outdated. Our focus is as much on interactions between children, their peers and adults as it is on interactions between children and technology so our observations will outlive particular toys or devices.

The research took place over a number of years, originally located in preschool settings and with a focus on enhancing practice and informing policy. An acknowledgement that the role of ICT in early childhood education was not being fully explored or exploited led to a commission to inform the development of the Scottish government's policy. Our review of the literature (Stephen and Plowman 2002) pointed to the paucity of good evidence-based writing on the subject. Indeed, despite claims about the powerful contribution that ICT could make to young children's learning and development, we were drawn to the conclusion that there were more questions than answers about that contribution, so we embarked on the observational study of existing practice mentioned earlier, *Come back in two years!*

This was followed by looking at the strategies that could be adopted by practitioners to enhance learning with ICT, and we later moved to examining experiences in the home. This transition from developing policy to examining practice to taking a broader view of the place of technology in the lives of young children mirrors the evolving areas of focus for policy makers – particularly how children's experiences with technology at home can contribute to their education. During the period spanned by our research, early years practitioners have been increasingly encouraged to value home learning, but they have not necessarily been aware of how children's experiences with technology at home can contribute to activities in the playroom and the early years of primary school. The research reported here describes the competences, knowledge and understanding that children develop at home by playing with technology and by being part of a family in which using technologies for domestic tasks, leisure, work or study are just everyday activities.

All of the participants in our research projects lived in Scotland's central belt. This area includes Edinburgh and Glasgow and comprises small towns with an industrial past, former mining villages and communities in rural and semi-rural settings. While some parts of the central belt have successfully made the transition from mining or manufacturing to service industries, others are in decline, with high levels of unemployment and limited opportunities for work. Preschool education is provided for children aged between three and five, with almost all four-year-old children (96 per cent) in part-time preschool education funded by the government and provided by the public, private or voluntary sectors (Scottish Government 2008b). The children in our studies attended nursery, typically for a morning or afternoon session, although some children attended on a wrap-around basis which extended to cover a typical working day.

Over the course of the research projects that provide the basis for this book we visited households and nurseries. We describe these various settings as well as interactions between children, family members and nursery staff. We refer to parents throughout this book, but this sometimes means adult caregivers who took a parental role in the household and were not necessarily biologically related to the children in their care; we also refer to other family members, such as siblings and grandparents, who had important roles in supporting and shaping children's learning. The appendices provide accounts of these research projects. They provide information on the nurseries and the case study families, explaining how they were identified and the nature of their involvement in the research. We also summarize our methods of data collection, with a particular emphasis on our approaches for eliciting children's perspectives. This section will be of interest to researchers and to readers who require more detail about the design and conduct of the research.

Our approach to discussing young children growing up with technology is firmly rooted in our research. Observations from multiple visits to preschools and family households enable us to build detailed portraits of children's lives, as illustrated by the vignettes in the Introduction and elsewhere. The interviews with adults enable us to add to this knowledge by gaining insights into their values and attitudes; conversations with children give us some insights into their preferences and choices. The research settings of home and preschool are conceptualized both as technological landscapes and as settings in which cultural values are modelled and transmitted through social relationships. By combining these ways of looking at children's daily lives with their families and in preschool settings, we can develop our understanding of their experiences with technology and how the attitudes and aspirations of their parents and practitioners can shape the nature and focus of their interactions. This enables us to move beyond those studies that focus on interactions between children and technologies without taking account of the broader context. These studies (some of which are described in Plowman and Stephen 2003) tend to look at individual children using computers in nursery or kindergarten settings, often with an emphasis on the development of operational skills, such as mouse control, or specific areas of the curriculum, such as children using electronic books to develop literacy. It also enables us to move beyond the fixed positions of those strongly against or in favour of the role of technology in early years education to provide a more nuanced account of the different kinds of learning that technology can support: we counter some of the assumptions about its deleterious effects while acknowledging the ways in which children can benefit from guided interaction and the ways in which they express their own preferences.

Growing up

Although we focus on just a year or so in the lives of the children and families in our studies, change is an important feature of their lives. Alexander (2006: 11) reminds us that development 'is a social process as well as a biological one'. Certainly, during the children's participation in the research, we observed rapid developmental change in terms of physical growth, motor skills, cognition and emotions, but we also saw dramatic changes in what they were allowed to do, the places they went and with whom they spent time. Because we visited families every couple of months over a year, we were able to document these changes. As nursery sessions are usually available for half days, many children of this age spend most of their time in the family household; this means that the values and attitudes of their parents are very influential in the experiences children have and the resources they encounter. As frequently pointed out, parents are the first and most enduring educators of their children and, whether they are aware of it or not, the home is the first learning environment, with or without technology.

Children in Scotland typically start school in the year in which they become five years old, so one of the key transitions for many of the children was beginning primary school towards the end of their period of participation in the research. As the transition to school approached, some parents not only endeavoured to prepare their children for changes to daily routines and new relationships, but they also became more attuned to their children's learning, mainly in terms of literacy and numeracy and seeing computers or toy laptops as offering opportunities for school readiness.

This was a period, then, in which children experienced diverse changes and parents saw an acceleration of growing up. Thinking about the future and a child's education is fundamental to a parent's role, but whereas psychologists tend to focus on developmental changes, sociological discussions about childhood are saturated by concepts of children 'being' or 'becoming'. Lee (2002) analyses the ways in which children are seen as the future, as human 'becomings' rather than human 'beings' who are agents in the construction of their own childhood. A child who is becoming is in training to become an adult and is deficient in the skills that confer adulthood. As Uprichard (2008) points out, the future orientation of the becoming discourse places more importance on what the child will become than what the child is, and risks overlooking the everyday nature of life as a child. It also associates competency with adulthood. But the more recent emphasis on being, in which children are seen as social actors and having agency, is also limited. Uprichard questions this distinction, seeing children as both being and becoming, suggesting that looking forward is an important part of being a child. In discussing children growing up with technology, we attempt to do both: a focus on technology makes a consideration of the future almost inevitable, and we share with parents and nursery staff an interest in these 'becoming' children's emerging skills, competences and dispositions, but we also recognize the wide range of competences that children have in the here and now.

The *Early Years Learning Framework for Australia* brings together the concepts of being and becoming with belonging. In its vision for children's learning, it states:

> *Belonging* is about knowing where and with whom we belong. A sense of belonging is integral to human existence. Children belong first to a family, within a cultural group, within a neighbourhood and to a wider community. Belonging acknowledges interdependence with others and the primacy of relationships in defining identities. In early childhood, relationships are critical to a sense of belonging. Belonging is central to being and becoming in that it shapes who children are and who they can become.
>
> *Being* is about the present, and of knowing ourselves, building and maintaining relationships with others, engaging with life's joys and complexities, and meeting challenges in everyday life. Childhood is not solely a preparation for adulthood or for the future – it is a time to be, to seek and make meaning of the world. Being recognizes the significance of the here and now in children's lives.
>
> *Becoming* is about the changes that occur in identities, knowledge, understandings, capacities, skills and relationships. It reflects the process of rapid and significant change that occurs in the early years as young children learn and grow. Becoming emphasises learning to participate fully and actively in society.
>
> (Commonwealth of Australia 2009: 4, original emphasis)

The above-cited document is designed to help practitioners plan, implement and evaluate the early years curriculum, and it is wide-ranging in its aspirations and scope. The document makes very little reference to digital technologies, but emphasizes the importance of families and educators working in partnership to support young children's learning and development. Our emphasis is on those aspects of children's everyday lives where encounters with technology provide opportunities to develop understandings of the world and the social and cultural roles of technology. We describe these aspects of everyday life in some detail in Chapter 6, along with the ways in which children can demonstrate agency by resisting suggestions or making their own preferences clear. Nevertheless, as the earlier discussion about government policy on technological skills for future education and employment indicates, children's experiences can be shaped by political and economic factors over which they have little control.

Towards the end of his book (which has the subtitle *Growing Up in an Age of Uncertainty*), Lee says:

> ... we seem to have said very little about growing up. There are some very good reasons for avoiding this topic entirely. It is still hard to think of children changing over time without accepting the terms of the dominant framework. This is because it seems hard to chart and to describe change unless one has a fixed finishing point, such as journey's end or standard, complete adulthood, to refer to.
>
> (Lee 2002: 137)

This suggests the need for some caution in using the title *Growing Up with Technology* for this book as we do not assume a 'fixed finishing point'. Rather, we use the title to suggest some of the changes that children, families and educators encounter in the year or two before starting compulsory schooling at five years old. The forward trajectory is implicit in our discussion of developing capacities and the imminence of school, but the focus on the role of technology in the lives of children and their families blurs some of these issues about being and becoming, the present and the future. While becoming children are seen as deficient in the competences they have yet to acquire as adults, such as reading and writing, we frequently heard adults say that children know more than they do when it comes to technology. So this is one area where children are not necessarily perceived by their parents or teachers to be incompetent. This is deemed worthy of comment because it seems surprising – after all, these children are three or four years old. It is only in this aspect of everyday life that parents perceive their child to know more than they do, even if these statements refer to basic operational procedures on a games console. The belief that children are more competent than adults in this arena can contribute to a feeling that technology is responsible for an inversion of the natural order, one where young children know more than their parents and assumptions about the meanings of both childhood and adulthood are troubled. But, as discussed later, at the same time that adults express inadequacy or a feeling of being threatened by this lack of knowledge, they also see technological proficiency as a natural state for children, such that children are believed to just 'pick up' their learning rather than it being transmitted in ways with which parents are more familiar (Plowman, McPake and Stephen 2008).

The view that children's accomplishment with technology is the norm is held in parallel with a belief that play is a natural activity for children. These phenomena of technology and play are sometimes oppositional, with parents expressing concerns about the ways in which technological pastimes detract from time available for play, which is seen as a healthier activity. At other times, these conflicting positions converge in the frequently used expression 'playing with the computer', which reduces the anxieties associated with the computer by seeing it as a plaything. As we see in Chapter 4, activities described in this way were rarely playful, at least in the nursery. This convergence of play and technological proficiency continues as children get older. It has led to a widespread belief, encapsulated in government plans to harness the power of computer games to accelerate learning, that what children learn through play will translate, over time, into skills needed for work and adult life. Hence we find expressions such as 'hard fun' or 'serious games' associated with learning with technology.

Technology

In its broadest sense, the word 'technology' can be used to mean the application of scientific knowledge and skills to extend human capabilities; as is frequently noted, this means that unremarkable items such as pencils can be described as technologies. However, we use the term in the way in which it is more commonly understood, certainly by the adult participants in our research, to refer to electronic objects that are found in homes and educational settings. To illustrate what we mean, by the time they started school, most of our case-study children had experience of using a broad range of technologies in their own homes and those of friends and relatives. They were likely to have access to toy mobile phones, laptops and cash registers and encounter a range of leisure technologies used by the family, such as interactive television and DVD players, electronic musical instruments, iPods and CD players. Digital and mobile phone cameras had an important role in communicating with friends and relatives beyond the immediate family, and children enjoyed use of the increasing range of games on computers, websites, games consoles, hand-held devices and mobile phones.

In his book *Beyond Technology*, Buckingham (2007: viii) writes that he regards some of the things we are interested in, such as computers and mobile phones, as media rather than technologies because he sees them as ways of representing the world and of communicating. While we share his interest in looking at these media in terms of social and cultural processes, we do not discuss approaches that are associated with study of the media, such as representation, textual analysis or means of production, and we generally use the term 'technologies' instead. This is not so much because we are specifically interested in machines or hardware (although we do make some observations about interface design and some of the operational difficulties that young children experience when interacting with computers), but because this is the term in common use and the materiality of these objects is particularly relevant for young children. Although we use 'ICT' to describe the information and communication technologies available in preschool, this is a term derived from policy and it is strongly associated with educational applications. Parents do not use this term, so we usually refer to 'technologies' in the home environment. We use the terminology in this way, shifting between the two, as it highlights the different types of technology and associated practices available in the two settings.

Shore (2008) calls for more research on how young children learn with digital media, the impact of adult participation and how children choose media experiences. Certainly, with some exceptions (Kirkorian, Wartella and Anderson 2008; Marsh *et al.* 2005; Rideout 2007), there have been few research-informed accounts of young children's uses of technologies to date. This is surprising in light of the public interest in this area, but is understandable in terms of some of the challenges of conducting research with preschoolers. Many of the anxieties about children's uses of technologies focus too narrowly on computers. While we are not aware of evidence to suggest computers are actively harmful, our research suggests that desktop computers do not appear to promote learning for three- and four-year-old children in situations where they are left to play on their own because preschool staff are busy and need to oversee many children and different activities. We outline some of the observations that led us to this conclusion as well as describe some ways in which adults or more able peers can guide interaction and enhance learning.

A restricted view of technology, such as a focus on desktop computers, can lead to a restricted view of play. We suggest thinking about technology more broadly, including digital still and video cameras, electronic keyboards and toys that simulate laptops and mobile phones. These technologies can provide better support for mobility and collaborative use, are easier to integrate into play activities, are more fun to use and can support a range of pursuits. Whether at home or in the nursery, this expanded range of technologies can also promote more opportunities for learning, especially an understanding of the cultural and social roles of technologies and the development of digital literacies.

Technology and identity

In their study of highly skilled information technology workers, McMullin, Comeau and Jovic (2007) describe the ways in which their participants defined themselves in terms of the technology they grew up with: the 'Console generation' was born between 1964 and 1973; the 'Windows generation' was born between 1974 and 1978; and the 'Internet generation' was born from 1979 on. It is too early to muse on the technologies that are likely to define the generation of children in our studies. Just in the few years since these children were born, we have seen the introduction of touch-screen mobile phones with integrated internet communications and music players, software that enables us to make telephone calls over the internet, the growth in podcasting, services which enable us to watch television programmes as streamed video content on computers and mobile devices, cloud computing and netbooks, the small laptop computers designed primarily for email and accessing the web. In *Future Issues in Socio-Technical Change for UK Education*, Cliff, O'Malley and Taylor (2008) speculate about possible transformations to our lives, considering developments in brain–machine interfaces, psychopharmocology and artificial intelligence as possible trends and suggesting that the biotechnology of synthetic life could have as much impact over the next 30 years as the personal computer did in the previous 30 years. They remind us that technological advances will inevitably change society but, in tandem, social factors shape and influence the research, development, commercialization and use of technology. Their analysis of technology trends suggests that it would be foolish to jump to conclusions about the technological futures that the young children who are three and four years old now are likely to inhabit.

In *Growing Up Digital*, another book with 'growing up' in the title, Tapscott (1998) refers to the 'Net Generation' (also 'N-generation' and 'N-geners'), so called because it is the first generation to grow up surrounded by digital media and their connections to the internet. He defines this generation as those who were between the ages of two and 22 in 1999, whether or not they were active users of the internet, although he cites figures that show that less than 30 per cent of households were expected to have online access at the time of the book's publication in 1998. Compare that to the most recent figures for Scotland (Office for National Statistics 2008), where the research for this book was carried out. They show that 61 per cent of households had internet access (slightly less than the figure for the UK as a whole, which was 65 per cent) and that, of these, more than 80 per cent had a broadband connection, which was generally not available at the time that Tapscott was writing. Although Tapscott includes children from the age of two in his definition of the Net Generation, the views and experiences of the young people in his study were participants in online forums which required a fairly high level of functional literacy. As with most commentators on digital generations, he does not take account of children as young as those we describe, and they are noticeable by their absence in most accounts of children's uses of technology.

Tapscott claims that motor skills, language and social skills, cognition, intelligence, reasoning and personality and, during adolescence, autonomy, a sense of the self and values are enhanced by interaction with technology. He declares that 'What we know for certain is that children without access to the new media will be developmentally disadvantaged' (op. cit.: 7). We do not share this certainty. Although the research we carried out was primarily focused on children's learning, we did not compare children using technology with those that did not and we did not assess learning gains or try to measure development. What we are interested in here is describing some of the forms of learning that we have identified, making a distinction between learning *about* technology and learning *with* technology, and examining the different forms this can take in the social and technological landscapes in which children spend time.

The concept of growing up is also central to 'digital natives', the term coined by Prensky (2001) to describe school and college students who have grown up with digital technology and speak its language. This is contrasted with 'digital immigrants', which describes people, such as their teachers, who have adopted technology later in life and learnt to adapt to their environment but do not assimilate fully. The terms have captured the popular imagination, perhaps because they simplify these generational differences and chime with the oft-stated belief, mentioned earlier, that children know more about technology than adults. We see greater complexity than this distinction implies. Visits to families where the parents were avid users of technology but the children were not force us to question how practices and preferences emerge. The use of 'natives' and 'immigrants' suggest identities that are determined by the technology, whereas, as this example suggests, both children and adults demonstrate their own preferences. Avoiding a technocentric approach by examining families' and practitioners' everyday experiences within a social and cultural framework shows that the metaphor is difficult to sustain. The metaphor does not follow through if we think of immigrants as energetic, ambitious and adventurous people who bring new cultures, new ways of doing things and new blood to an established country. The use of the term 'digital natives' suggests that digital culture is a place that belongs to the young but has been colonized by the old, but our research evidence suggests that this is too simplistic.

We do not see the children in our studies as defined by the prevailing technologies, so we do not give them tags such as 'digital natives', 'technotots', 'toddler netizens' or 'digikids'. Our research shows that technology is not a defining feature of their lives, but is just one of a range of activities in which they engage on their own or with their families. This being the case, it prompts a question about why we would want to write a book on the topic. The political commitment to the introduction of ICT described earlier means that practitioners are now expected to offer technological resources to support children's learning, but we know that there are uncertainties and misapprehensions, some of which are shared by parents. Our aim is to contribute to debates about the value and desirability of young children using computers and to enable others to engage in conversations and come to some conclusions about the following questions. Is it important for children of this age to learn to use technology? Are some children in a better position than others to take advantage of it? What is best suited to their needs? Children come to preschool with different experiences from home. How can practitioners recognize and extend these experiences? Many of the perceived benefits of technology concern children's learning, but hitherto there has been little analysis of the kinds of learning that technology supports or impedes for children in this age range. We have developed different categories of learning with and through technology that are based on our observations and practitioners' accounts, which allow us to explore these issues. We return to these questions in Chapter 9 and reflect on the evidence that we have presented from our research.

The structure of the book

Following on from the point we make here – that educators should be aware of, and engage in, discussions about technologies and young children – Chapter 2 looks at some of the different positions that are taken on this emotive topic. Evangelists promote the benefits of video games and romanticize a techno-logical future, but other commentators romanticize a non-technological past and are cautious, seeing the technologization of childhood as detracting from social and imaginative play and contributing to obesity. The currency of the metaphor of a 'toxic childhood' and recent reports which provide a gloomy prognosis for contemporary childhood indicate the scale of anxieties.

We trace two of the main theories that have influenced how we now understand young children's learning in Chapter 3, looking at the ideas initially developed by Piaget and Vygotsky. We explain key concepts such as interaction and pedagogy, and we explain how we see learning as taking place within a sociocultural framework, considering the extent to which play is a medium for learning for young children and describing what we know about the role of technology in play and learning at home and preschool. Technology is both a part of the context which influences children's learning outcomes and is one of the cultural tools which children make their own as they learn.

Chapters 4 and 5 provide more detailed discussions of learning in preschool, looking at how the use of technology relates to policy, curriculum and pedagogy. These chapters look at the practitioners' perspectives and why they are often ambivalent about the role of technology in early years settings: they acknowledge the demands of the curriculum and the need to prepare children for school and later life, but they are also uncertain about what this means for their own professional practice. Picture sequences based on video evidence of the problems children encounter when using computers lead to a discussion of why this matters for children's learning and why many of these problems might be reduced if children are given opportunities to engage with more diverse forms of ICT.

The chapters examine the ways in which pedagogy can evolve as ICT becomes an established feature of playrooms. We describe how we enrolled practitioners in a process of guided enquiry. This led to us jointly identifying ways of supporting children's interactions with technology that were consistent with the ethos of the playroom and the development of our understanding of guided interaction. This approach to thinking about pedagogy was informed by the understanding of learning outlined in Chapter 3 and builds on existing practices in the playroom rather than allowing technology to drive educational change. The concept of guided interaction is introduced and positioned in relation to sociocultural theories of how learning can be supported by other, more able helpers through scaffolding and guided participation. Help can be provided by adults (e.g. practitioners or family members) or other children (e.g. siblings or peers), but the prevalence of this help and the forms it takes vary from one context to another. The practitioners' interventions enabled us to analyse learning with technology in more detail than hitherto, leading to a categorization of learning with and through technology as (i) extending knowledge of the world, (ii) acquiring operational skills and (iii) developing dispositions to learn. We present tables which provide examples of these different types of learning in relation to a detailed description of guided interaction broken down into the different types of support, the different modes in which that support is enacted and the type of learning with which the support is associated, and describe the ways in which it can be integrated into practice on a day-to-day basis.

Chapter 6 moves away from preschool settings to look at what is known about learning in the home, and then goes on to consider the home as an environment for learning about and with technology. It looks at the home in terms of its physical features, family practices, family values and family interactions, using survey and case-study data to build pictures of parents' expectations and aspirations for their children's futures as users of technology. Chapter 7 examines the three forms of learning with technology that we have identified in preschool settings but in the context of the home and adds (iv) learning about technologies as cultural practices. The domestic and leisure technologies with which children play or observe in use at home are conceptualized as environmental technologies that can encourage extended forms of learning, including the development of digital literacies. Chapter 8 contrasts this with what is available in preschool settings and discusses some of the ways in which young children's encounters with technologies are supported in these different environments. It outlines the various ways in which guided interaction can be provided and the types of learning that are found in these different technological and sociocultural landscapes.

Chapter 9 returns to the questions posed earlier in this chapter: Is it important for children of this age to learn to use technology? Are some children in a better position than others to take advantage of it? What is best suited to their needs? How can preschool practitioners recognize and extend these experiences? It considers the transition from preschool to school by looking to the future of these children, considering whether the recent policy emphasis on home learning means that some families are disadvantaged in terms of children's opportunities to use technologies. It considers what forms these digital divides take, and whether their impact persists as children start their formal education in school. Understanding children's experiences across different contexts enables us to identify ways in which their prior learning can be supported and their rich experiences of different technologies can be acknowledged so that they are prepared for the technological futures that face them. Finally, in the Conclusion, we return to Evie and Andy, the children introduced in the Introduction, to get a glimpse of their experiences after they started school.

Chapter 2

The technologization of childhood?

Over the last decade or so, the increasing pervasiveness of domestic and leisure technologies has led to public debate about their role in the lives of young children. This debate has arisen in part because some organizations and pressure groups have expressed anxieties about children's health and well-being which have been picked up by the media. The issues have intensified and gained momentum, and most parents have some level of awareness of the key issues. Although we found evidence of some parental disquiet about the role of technology in children's lives, we also found that families did not assimilate these views unthinkingly; they made their own choices based on their own values and family circumstances. Overall, technology was not perceived by parents to be the threat to modern childhood that media coverage leads us to believe it is, but we discuss some of the main features of these debates here as they form a backdrop to the studies we describe. The role of parenting is central in these debates. According to those who allude to the crisis in childhood, parents have abdicated responsibility for protecting their children from the dangers presented by technology. Long working hours mean that screen-based media are used as babysitters by parents who are too tired or too busy to engage with their children in more acceptable ways, they say. For those who maintain that these same technologies are beneficial, parents are castigated for failing to acknowledge the ways in which they provide intellectual challenge and opportunities for learning.

Commentators on both sides of the argument hold strong beliefs which tend to be based on a partisan interpretation of evidence, where it exists. Assertions are made on the basis of anecdote or personal experience, but these assertions are presented as having a stronger evidence base than this. In her introduction to a report on the risks children face from the internet and video games, Byron (2008: 1) refers to a 'fiercely polarised debate in which panic and fear often drown out evidence'. Although exponents of toxicity tend to get more media coverage than advocates of technology's merits, we present here a brief account of both sides of the argument. We see those who fear the role of technologies in children's lives as romanticizing the past, because they tend to look back on a golden age of childhood, before technology was as pervasive as it is now. The enthusiasts for technology tend to romanticize the future, projecting its benefits for children into their future lives as students and employees.

Romanticizing the past

Successive generations have given prominence to the expression of anxieties about the ways in which childhood is being transformed in undesirable ways, each time focusing on the latest technology. Young children are seen as vulnerable to adverse influences, and it is claimed that their cognitive, emotional and social development is threatened by technology. The discussion usually centres on the dominance of screen-based media (e.g. television, games consoles and computers) in children's lives, and how this leads to a number of ills, including social isolation and obesity (Plowman, McPake and Stephen in press). These threats fall into three main categories, relating to: health and well-being, cognition and effects on the brain and the social and cultural aspects of children's lives.

Until recently, the debate was most strongly expressed in the United States. The American Academy of Pediatrics Committee on Public Education has published guidelines on young children's exposure to the media and recommends that pediatricians should urge parents to: avoid television viewing for children under the age of two, make children's rooms 'electronic media-free environments' and resist using the media as electronic babysitters. In the interests of being good role models, they suggest that pediatricians should also limit the use of television and videos in patients' waiting rooms and that they should provide educational materials to promote reading (American Academy of Pediatrics Committee on Public Education 1999: 342). They have also warned against the effects of media violence in television programmes, music and video games (2001), although claims and counter-claims about the effects of television have a long history.

Media effects research was originally associated with television but has since been extended to encompass the effects of digital media. The reported studies are usually large scale and so have considerable influence with the general public, although they also have shortcomings. Oakes (2009) offers a critique, pointing out that such studies tend to focus on age and gender, but rarely look at outcomes for different social groups and do not take fully into account the context of use. Anderson and Hanson (2009) comment on the ways in which media exposure is typically correlated with outcomes, implying a causal connection which may not exist. Effects research generally makes connections between media use and what are seen as undesirable outcomes; it is rarely interested in possible links between media use and desirable outcomes. Similarly, those who fear a technologization of childhood tend to focus on what they see as the unwelcome outcomes of exposure to technologies.

Many of the views promoted by the Alliance for Childhood, based in the United States but with partner organizations elsewhere, are uncontroversial.

They publicize the benefits of child-initiated play and high quality child education programmes, for instance, but also express concerns about the potential harm of computers. In *Fool's Gold: A Critical Look at Computers in Childhood* (Cordes and Miller 2000) the Alliance for Childhood called for an immediate halt to the further introduction of computers in early childhood, except for special cases of students with disabilities. It recommended a refocusing on 'the essentials of a healthy childhood' (e.g. play, reading books and 'hands-on experiences of nature and the physical world') and urged the Surgeon General to produce a report on the hazards computers pose to children. It was followed by *Tech Tonic: Towards a New Literacy of Technology* which described technology as responsible for irreversible changes in human biology, claiming that:

> the damage being done by immersing children in electronic technologies is becoming clearer. Increasing numbers of them spend hours each day sitting in front of screens instead of playing outdoors, reading, and getting much-needed physical exercise and face-to-face social interaction—all of which, it turns out, also provide essential stimulation to the growing mind and intellect
>
> (Alliance for Childhood 2004: 1)

The report promoted education as a means of inspiring and preparing children to protect the world's ecology and make wise choices in the future, stating that 'It is time for concerted citizen action to reclaim childhood for children' (op. cit.: 1). Other concerns are voiced by those such as Bruner and Bruner (2006: xxi), who refer to video games as the 'digital drug' and warn parents of the dangers of addiction, and Sigman (2007), who refers to the malign influence of television and the ways in which children are 'remotely controlled' by it. The addictive nature of technologies is also explored in *The Plug-In Drug* (Winn 2002), which claims that children get 'hooked' on television and computers.

Buckingham (2000) describes positions such as these as adopting a 'death of childhood' thesis in which it is believed that childhood has been lost as a result of changes in modern society. Postman (1982/1994), for instance, refers to technology as causing the disappearance of childhood. Fuelled by a combination of panic and nostalgia, fears about young children's use of technology have persisted over the last few decades and exist in an assortment of undifferentiated anxieties about childhood. An example of this convergence of concerns in the UK is found in a letter published in the *Daily Telegraph* newspaper with over one hundred signatories, including well-known children's authors, academics and clinicians. Headed 'Modern life leads to more depression among children' the letter goes on to say:

> Since children's brains are still developing, they cannot adjust – as full-grown adults can – to the effects of ever more rapid technological and

cultural change. They still need what developing human beings have always needed, including real food (as opposed to processed 'junk'), real play (as opposed to sedentary, screen-based entertainment), first-hand experience of the world they live in and regular interaction with the real-life significant adults in their lives.

(Abbs and others, 2006)

This letter prompted widespread commentary in the media and the metaphor of a 'toxic childhood', used in the eponymous book (Palmer 2006), became strongly associated with this debate. The book, the subtitle of which is 'How the modern world is damaging our children and what we can do about it', includes sections on additives in food, the decline of family mealtimes and good manners, the lack of outdoor play and changes in children's sleeping habits. Palmer refers to 'the damage that can be inflicted on children by a competitive, consumer-driven, screen-based lifestyle' (op. cit.: xiii) and states that 'the world we've created is damaging our children's brains' (op. cit.: 308). The 'technology-driven culture' (op. cit.: 3) in which we live means that:

Many [children] spend at least as much of their leisure time on screen-based activities as they do with the real people in their lives. So what children watch on TV, film and DVD and what they do on computers and console games clearly affects their development.

(Palmer 2006: 227)

As we saw in Chapter 1, Tapscott (1998) claimed with certainty that children *without* access to the new media will be developmentally disadvantaged. In contrast, we find here that Palmer is equally certain that children *with* access to these same technologies are exposed to the same risks of being developmentally disadvantaged. Most of these commentators take a view on the relationship between technology and children's development, referring to its adverse effect on growing minds and developing brains. But proving a causal link between developmental delay and technology is not possible when technology takes so many different forms and commentators elide nutrition, opportunities for play, sleep patterns, lifestyle, family stability and parental roles as facets of modern life that lead to this danger. The aspects of daily life that we saw and the views of parents that we elicited suggest a need for more caution in the conclusions that we draw. We found a more ambiguous situation, one in which parents had some uncertainties and were aware of some of the arguments but still felt mainly comfortable about the decisions they had made regarding their child's use of technologies. Nevertheless, these anxieties about the role of technology endure. In *Under Pressure*, Honoré (2008) reiterates many of the arguments of Palmer's *Toxic Childhood*, citing electronic toys and screen-based media as responsible for a range of ills and suggesting that a return to forms of parenting associated with previous generations can rescue children.

A Good Childhood: Searching for Values in a Competitive Age (Layard and Dunn 2009) is the report of an enquiry commissioned by The Children's Society charity as a reaction to what it sees as a childhood in crisis. In the report summary on lifestyle, it provides some figures on the numbers of children over five years old who have their own mobile phone or television and refers to the serious problems brought about by new technologies.

The focus of these concerns is often on young children because they are seen as innocent and particularly vulnerable in the early stages of development. A commonly held – but often implicit – position is that technology is necessary for adults' leisure time and essential for their working lives, but it is unsuitable for young children. Cars, mobile telephones and microwave ovens are occasionally the subject of public concern, but they are such an integral part of adults' lives that there are few serious suggestions that their use should be curtailed. The problems with technologies are therefore typically couched in terms which acknowledge the benefits for those old enough and wise enough to appreciate them while obliging adults to protect children from their harmful effects.

As will be discussed further in Chapter 3, the risks to children's learning are concerned with what is perceived to be developmentally appropriate. Healy (1998), for instance, claims that the early years are a 'busy time for the brain' and that using computers before the age of seven subtracts from important developmental tasks. However, the risks to children's intellectual development are not generally seen as the main source of anxiety. Many parents consider that technology can provide a number of benefits for their children's learning; the risks that have greater dominance in the public discourse are concerned with other areas of children's lives. Health and well-being are seen as under threat because it is widely believed that children spend too much time indoors and that the sedentary lifestyle encouraged by these products increases the risk of obesity. Perceptions that children ignore or reject activities that are considered to be healthier because they spend too much time playing computer games or watching television have led to the language of addiction (i.e. being hooked, drug, controlled, etc.) being used to describe their effects.

Another set of concerns focuses on social and cultural issues. Some observers consider that opportunities for family interaction are curtailed and children's social development is at risk because children are believed to play computer and video games on their own and for long periods of time, leading to threats to their linguistic development and inhibition of their imagination and creativity. Honoré (2008: 104), for instance, claims that 'Too many screen hours can deny young children the real-life, hands-on interaction with people and objects that is essential for their development'. As a consequence, it is believed, children become sleep deprived, their behaviour deteriorates and they are reported as having tantrums when parents try to limit their computer activities. There are also concerns that extended use of the internet and television can increase the likelihood of children's exposure to unsuitable content and that it contributes to the commercialization of childhood as advertisers prey on susceptible children. While young children are generally seen as particularly vulnerable, they are not exposed to all the dangers threatening older children: three- and four-year-old children who do not read and write are not as likely to stray into chat rooms or unsuitable websites, for instance.

The position taken, either implicitly or explicitly, is that children and their families did not have to contend with these problems in some unspecified golden period of childhood that existed in the past. Adults seem ready to romanticize their own childhoods in terms of outdoor play, an always-shining sun and lots of social interaction with friends. Children then – whenever 'then' was – enjoyed a carefree childhood in which they shared board games, were absorbed in art and craft activities and wholesome hobbies, role played in homemade dressing-up clothes and read books.

However, variants of the risks associated with modern toxic childhoods were prevalent for earlier generations, even if the technologies and cultural activities were different. Known as moral panics, these expressions of anxieties about changes to social order can be associated with groups of young people, such as mods and rockers in the 1960s or punks in the late 1970s, or ascribed to the power of new technologies to threaten stability and the well-being of families and children. Postman (op. cit.: 149) states that 'sustained, articulate, and mature speech is almost absent from the airwaves' because he fears that radio had been usurped by competition from television. This fear of change has a long history. Several hundred years BC, in the *Phaedrus*, Plato (2005) reflected concerns that people would lose the power of memory because writing things down meant dispensing with the need to remember them. He described the god Theuth's invention of letters as being a drug for memory and wisdom, recalling the language of those who are now concerned about the addictive nature of television and computer games. In the latter part of the eighteenth century and early years of the nineteenth century, increases in women's literacy led to concerns about young women reading novels in case it should make them unsatisfied with their situations and neglect their duties (Pearson 1999).

Romanticizing the future

The anxieties about technology fell into three main categories: health and well-being, cognition and effects on the brain and the social and cultural aspects of children's lives. Protagonists for the positive power of technologies such as computer and video games tend to focus on the latter two categories and ignore the first; claims for the ways in which these technologies contribute to children's health and well-being are not prominent. However, the introduction of the Nintendo Wii has led to a more physically active approach to using games consoles and the role of these technologies in supporting health and well-being is now being more heavily promoted.

Books with titles such as *How Computer Games Help Children Learn* (Shaffer 2007), *Good Video Games + Good Learning* (Gee 2007), *Don't Bother me Mom – I'm Learning!* (Prensky 2006) and even *Everything Bad is Good for You: Why popular culture is making us smarter* (Johnson 2006) promote the view that concerns about computers are misguided. It is noticeable that many of the perceived benefits of children's uses of technologies relate to learning and cognition. All four of these books have 'learning' (or a synonym of it) in their titles and make the case that computers develop a range of competences. The thinking skills developed by computer games and other digital media include, according to Prensky (2006: 35), competence in reading visual images as representations of three-dimensional space, the ability to create mental maps, inductive discovery, such as making observations and formulating hypotheses, and the ability to focus on several things at the same time and respond quickly to unexpected stimuli. In *What Video Games Have to Teach Us about Learning and Literacy*, Gee (2003) itemizes 36 learning principles, including promoting the ability to connect different sign systems, problem solving, understanding nonverbal cues and transferring skills from one task to another.

Schools and parents, it is claimed, need to catch up with these new skills and literacies. The emphasis is not on the past, but on a future in which children will flourish as a result of their interactions with technology, particularly video and computer games: 'Kids learn more positive, useful things for their future from their video games than they learn in school!' (Prensky 2006: 4).

Shaffer, Squire, Halverson and Gee (2005: 110–111) claim that schools are still stuck with traditional academic disciplines that originated in mediaeval times and have not changed much since the Industrial Revolution. Classrooms have not adapted to the demands of a 'postindustrial, global, high tech society' and so school is 'increasingly seen as irrelevant by many students who are past the primary grades'. By interacting with simulated worlds, it is possible for students to develop ways of thinking that are valued in the adult workplace; they suggest using learning theory to design games for future scientists, engineers, lawyers and other professionals. Shaffer (2007) describes how video and computer games help children to build successful futures.

In this respect, these authors share an interest with the government policies (outlined in Chapter 1) which aim to maximize the value of informal learning – at home and elsewhere – and use technology to prepare children for work in the knowledge economies of the future. *Their Space: Education for a digital generation*, a report for the think tank Demos, supports the argument in *Everything Bad is Good for You*: popular culture has become more complex and intellectually challenging. The report describes how:

> In an economy driven by knowledge rather than manufacturing, employers are already valuing very different skills, such as creativity, communication, presentation skills and team-building. Schools are at the

front line of this change and need to think about how they can prepare young people for the future workplace.

(Green and Hannon 2007: 15)

Opportunities to develop relationships with other children from around the world and strengthen notions of citizenship and global awareness are cited as social and cultural benefits by Jenkins, Clinton, Purushotma, Robison and Weigel (2006). They describe different forms of participatory culture as including affiliations (through membership of online communities), expressions (in terms of producing new creative forms) and collaborative problem solving. As such, it is clear that this analysis is more appropriate for older children and the report is based on teenagers' uses of digital technologies. Advocacy of the learning benefits of virtual worlds tends to be promoted more for older children than for preschoolers. This is partly because commentators such as Gee are interested in how schools can better prepare children for their futures and also because preschool-aged children's participation in these participatory cultures is limited by their emerging literacy and lack of exposure to these virtual worlds. There has been rapid growth in online virtual worlds for children aged six and above, such as Club Penguin, Neopets and Webkinz, but we very rarely found evidence of younger children using these sites.

The parents' views

What, then, were the views of the parents we contacted? They reported that the children in our case studies had different play preferences. We found that the role of technology in this play varied depending on availability, parental attitudes and individual disposition. All of the children in our case-study families, whether high or low users of technology, engaged in an extensive range of non-technological activities, such as small world play, dressing up and outdoor games: all but four children reported going to the park as one of their favourite activities; nearly all children regularly played outside in the street or garden; more than half of the children liked to go swimming. For some children, technology did not feature in their favourite activities at all. Sometimes these activities blended seamlessly: one boy liked to download and print images of characters from Lord of the Rings websites, stick them onto cardboard, cut them out and then role play with them alongside 3-D toys of characters from the film. Although we found that children's behaviour was shaped by family practices and theories about good parenting, our evidence suggests that children's individual preferences, interests and dispositions were also important influences, and we found that children were discriminating users of technology (Stephen, McPake, Plowman and Berch-Heyman 2008). Children who lived in 'high technology' homes were not necessarily drawn to use these resources, regardless of the activities or invitations of their parents or siblings.

Practices such as purchasing decisions, the kinds of technologies which children were allowed to use and the balance struck between technological and traditional toys and activities were influenced not so much by income as by family values. Parents were not necessarily explicitly concerned with learning outcomes derived from technological activities – although they often became more aware of educational potential as their child's transition to school became imminent – but they had an interest in supporting the development of operational skills (e.g. finding specific websites) so that their children could become independent users and occupy themselves. Parents also taught children to use a television remote control for the same purpose: it was described as 'mum and dad's best friend' by one parent. While some television programmes were seen to have learning value, parents felt less guilty about using the computer because the act of using it was perceived to be educational. Only nine per cent of the 346 parents responding to the survey disagreed with the statement 'I expect the internet to play an important part in my child's education'; other responses showed that playing with the computer was seen as a preparation for using the internet more actively as children get older.

Parental attitudes

Across these case-study families, there was no clear divide in attitudes between those who were economically advantaged or disadvantaged or even, in many cases, between 'high technology' and 'low technology' families; we found a stronger link between parents' own experiences of technology and how this influenced the opportunities they offered their children (McPake, Plowman and Stephen forthcoming). On our second visit to the families, participants responded to a set of statements which had been derived from our earlier interviews or some of the views expressed by the commentators above. These were presented on laminated cards and parents indicated whether they agreed or not. Their responses indicated that they had some concerns about their children's uses of technology but considered that their child was not at risk if it was used in moderation and with appropriate levels of supervision.

While a quarter of the parents agreed with the statement 'Using some kinds of technology can be damaging to children's health and development', most were uncertain and took the opportunity to discuss some of their concerns. Their comments referred to mobile phones, computer games and televisions, and the most frequently cited anxieties were about health and physical development, with some concerns about the potential impediment to social interaction and exposure to inappropriate content. However, the key feature of these responses was the extent to which they expressed reservations and uncertainty (e.g. 'studies say contradicting things', 'everything has its place in moderation' and 'I both agree and disagree') and the occasional difference of views between the mother and the father. This equivocation was also found when parents were presented with the statement 'Playing on the computer or PlayStation is just harmless fun'. While they broadly agreed with this statement, their agreement was qualified (e.g. 'yes, to a certain degree', 'yes – if not for too long' and 'yeah, as long as they're not doing it all day') and there were some comments about the need for regulation (e.g. 'fine within limits' and 'not more than one or two hours in one go').

The same statements were used on two different occasions about 15 months apart so that we could establish whether views altered. This period was characterized by many changes, both in the child's development and in the family environment. By the time of the second occasion, there was less uncertainty and more polarization of views. The balance had shifted to greater caution, perhaps reflecting the children's increased independence and, in some cases, ability to enter or read text, but responses about use of the computer or games consoles were still qualified (e.g. 'with parental controls', 'as long as it has its place', 'within reason', 'as long as it's limited' and 'depending on how it is used and how much time it is used for').

Regulation

As this feedback indicates, parents became more aware of potential problems as their children got older and they began to take steps to regulate use. Their main concerns were to achieve balance in their child's activities, introduce notional time limits and ensure some level of supervision. In response to the statement 'Playing computer games is one of my child's favourite activities', a third of parents agreed and a half of parents disagreed, with a slight increase in the numbers enjoying computer games by the end of the visits. None of the children was using technologies to a degree that worried parents. Nevertheless, all families, apart from one, agreed with the statement 'If children are playing with interactive toys, electronic games or new technologies they are missing out on more important activities'. The solution for the vast majority was to balance the amount of time spent on different pursuits, but parents were also keen to ensure an even distribution of indoor and outdoor activities and solo and social activities.

During an interview in the last visit, parents were asked if they had made any rules relating to their child's use of technology. More than half of the families referred to regulating use of the television, but only two mentioned regulating use of the computer: for some, it was not considered necessary because their child had no interest in using it. Rules about watching television were associated with times of the day when it could be watched, rather than the duration of viewing sessions, and this coincided with scheduling of suitable programmes. Typically children were allowed some time in the morning before going to nursery and some time before and after teatime, with a cut-off point of when they got ready for bed, although in several households the television was on for much of the day as a backdrop to family activities. About half the families allowed children to watch television on their own in their bedrooms and a couple of the children watched DVDs or video to go to sleep, but some parents only sanctioned viewing as a shared activity in a family room.

Some children needed to gain permission to use the computer or had to be supervised while using it, and a couple of families limited use of the printer because of the costs of replacement ink cartridges. Where there were rules, use of the computer was restricted by duration rather than time of day, although this was enforced flexibly. A reasonable period of time was typically seen as an hour or so, unless other family members wanted access.

The least ambivalence was found in response to 'I think that we have got the use of new technologies right for our child' as all respondents except one agreed with this statement. The parent who demurred felt that they should provide more for their child: 'I think there are some other things we could provide to give them more opportunities – like those handheld games. Perhaps Santa will bring these things.' Prompted by these statements, some parents expressed disapprobation of the extent to which others had got it right (e.g. 'some parents . . .', 'we would never allow that' and 'not our own children') suggesting that, even if these responses were not entirely consistent with their own family practices, they were aware of what would be seen as responsible parenting within the context of debates about children's uses of technology. There was a widespread belief that 'moderation' or 'a sensible balance' would guard against dangers, but there was substantial variation in practices from one family to another, so the ways in which this was interpreted varied.

Towards the end of the family visits many of the children started school, some were learning to read and write and some families had acquired internet access, computers, new mobile phones or portable DVD players. But the increase in the number of technological devices did not necessarily lead to increased use by the children. For those at school, there was less time available for play at home. And as they became more adept at independent play and as their skills at reading, writing and drawing increased, they found other ways of spending their time. Rideout (2007: 4) finds that concerns about adverse effects of media increase as children get older so, in time, perhaps these parents will find policing their children's activities more challenging. But, for now, parents mainly feel confident in their abilities to manage the use of technologies.

A technologized childhood?

Childhood experiences often shape how adults act as parents, but the technologies currently available for children were not part of their parents' upbringing. The lack of a model to inform this aspect of their parenting means that it is unexplored territory for a whole generation of parents and perhaps accounts for some of their uncertainty. Nevertheless, parents felt that they had things about right. We found no evidence to suggest that the childhoods of these children could be described as toxic in the ways outlined by media commentators and lobbyists or that family life was being undermined. It was not the technologies that determined whether a family communicated, played together or supported their child's learning, but their cultural practices and values. Our analysis indicated that a number of factors which are linked with, but not dependent on, socioeconomic status has a bearing on parental perspectives on young children's uses of technology. So although parents' attitudes were influenced by media discussions, they were also shaped by their educational background and prior experiences of using technologies for work, study or leisure purposes (McPake *et al.*, op. cit.). These findings are in line with recent research which has identified family practices as typically more influential than simple gender or class distinctions in the educational preparation of preschool children (Vincent *et al.* 2004).

We should point out that the parents who chose to participate in our studies were likely to be disposed towards providing a balanced and thoughtful upbringing for their children regardless of socioeconomic status, but our findings on parental attitudes and family practices are consistent with other research. In the UK, a survey of over 1,800 parents of children under six (Marsh *et al.* 2005: 5) found that children were considered to lead generally well-balanced lives, with popular culture, media and new technologies playing 'an important, but not overwhelming, role in their leisure activities'. A Kaiser Family Foundation report, based on a series of focus groups and a survey of over 1,000 parents with children aged six months to six years old, found that 'Many parents find media a tremendous benefit in parenting and can't imagine how they'd get through the day without it' (Rideout and Hamel 2006: 32). Anand and Krosnick (2005) conducted multiple regressions predicting time spent watching television, watching videos/DVDs, reading, playing video games and using computers using the Kaiser Family Foundation data. They found that parents' education (and marital status, which we did not use as a variable) had significant effects across most types of media use but family income had no impact at all. Although we acknowledge Morrow's (2006: 94) claim that 'family practices are deeply gendered', we did not find clear differences based on gender for these young children. Rideout and Hamel (2006: 27) refer to 'only modest differences' in patterns of use for children aged six years or under, and Anand and Krosnick (2005) found that gender had only occasional, isolated effects.

There seems to be a disjunction, then, between the case put forward by those warning of the toxic effects of technology and parents' own perceptions. While not a major source of anxiety, many parents were unsure how to respond to what some saw as contradictory accounts reported in the media. Parents were aware of some of the concerns expressed about technologies, but they were not troubled by them and nobody was worried about their own child's patterns of use. Nevertheless, the responses to the prepared statements were characterized by uncertainty and, sometimes, inconsistency. Although, overall, parents were happy with the role of technologies in their children's lives, they frequently qualified their position or referred to the need for moderation and limits. They used their judgement, sometimes sought advice and sometimes wondered if they had the right balance, but generally felt that they were on the right track. Beliefs that they should regulate their children's use of technology are not surprising given that parents have to supervise many of their young children's activities, including outdoor play (multiple potential dangers), painting and craft activities (messy) and even social encounters with friends (potential disagreements and being led astray). From this perspective, technological play may be seen as safer, in part because it takes place indoors, usually within the parents' peripheral vision (Plowman, McPake and Stephen 2008).

The broad range of technologies to which children have access or exposure may suggest that there has been a technologization of childhood if we ascribe agency to the technology. Such approaches are a response to each generation's fears about cultural change and are generally predicated on a view of children as lacking in agency. In our discussion of romanticizing the past we saw the prevalence of notions of a 'technology-driven culture' (Palmer 2006: 3), in which technology, among other agents, is responsible for making childhood 'toxic'. This technological determinism is at odds with the findings from our case studies, which suggest that children (and their parents) are active rather than passive users of technology, that an increase in technological items in the home does not necessarily lead to an increase in use by children and that a range of factors influences the ways in which technology is appropriated within a family setting.

Chapter 3

Young children learning

What is learning?

Learning can happen in any situation that young children encounter. Indeed, learning seems to be a pervasive feature of their lives: children learn in and out of educational settings, at home, in the playground, with others and sometimes when exploring alone. Perhaps it is this pervasiveness that makes it difficult to write a definition of learning that encompasses its many forms. For some, learning is synonymous with development and is something which happens as cognitive structures or ways of thinking mature and develop (e.g. as children learn the rules of their first spoken language). Others see learning as changes in the ways in which individuals participate in the world around them, interacting with people and objects with increased competence and independence; this form of learning can be seen when children learn to join in games with peers or take part in family activities and discussions.

In the research reported in this book, we have thought about learning as a process which is unseen but made evident by changes in children's level of skill, confidence or knowledge. Children learn how to do things (e.g. ride a bike or climb to the top of the slide), they learn to do things better (e.g. use cutlery or take turns) and they learn about the world in which they live (e.g. by identifying and categorizing animals, knowing about quantity or beginning to read). These three forms of learning can be found in our observations of children's encounters with technology and in their teachers' and parents' accounts of their progress. For instance, in the nursery there were examples of children learning how to use the controls on a tape recorder or the functions of a computer. At home, children learnt how to find the television programme they wished to watch or to answer a call on a mobile phone. Some of the practitioners' notes described children learning to do things better, for instance becoming able to print independently. Parents talked about their child's growing concentration on and persistence with games on the home computer. At preschool, children demonstrated that they were learning about the world when they used their knowledge to succeed in matching and sorting games or to describe patterns (e.g. fast and slow, soft and loud) in the music they were making. Similarly, at home they gathered information as they played hand-held games, began to read names on files on the computer screen and shared family stories and relationships as they reviewed digital photographs. To illustrate young children learning about and with technology, we have drawn together some examples that have been taken from field notes or extracted from interviews with parents and education professionals.

Learning about and with technology in the nursery

Simon managed the start, rewind and stop controls.

Fraser knew where to click to draw and print independently.

Cal's mouse control was sketchy, he needed support to follow the programme. But four days later his mouse control improved and he remembered how to log in and how to change the game.

Lizzy was able to drag puzzle pieces very easily. The adult's hand was pushed away when help was offered.

Ben, Simon and Lillian learn to relate the story heard to the pages in the book. Ben resists turning the page until the story has started and he hears the cue. Lillian notices when a page is skipped.

Learning about and with technology at home

Finn knows how to look at photos on his Mum's phone.

Jill has learnt how to play her favourite game on the CBeebies website.

After Mum arranges icons on the desktop for her, Fiona can choose and play games independently.

Arthur uses the interactive TV. He needs Mum to read any text, but he then plays alone while she does other things.

Christopher learnt about Portugal with his mother and sister when they looked at websites to prepare for a holiday.

Learning about the world, how to do things and how to do things better happens in the cognitive, social and emotional spheres of children's lives. Cognitive learning covers aspects sometimes described as intellectual or requiring mental action; it involves thinking, using language, categorizing, sequencing, storing and retrieving information. It is evident when children begin to be able to sort objects by colour, size and function or associate particular characteristics with objects or people. Using icons for navigation on a website, 'reading' a name or logo or being able to talk about a specific topic are all examples of activities which rely on cognitive learning. Learning in the social sphere is demonstrated when children start to negotiate shared roles and rules as they play together and when they acquire patterns of social behaviour that are appropriate for particular contexts, such as in preschool, at a friend's house or when shopping with parents. Emotional learning is seen when a child becomes able to manage separation from their parents or can empathize with the feelings of others and predict and describe his own reactions.

Table 3.1 sets out some of the competences that children typically acquire between the ages of three and five. In common with Weigel, James and Gardner

Table 3.1 Characteristics of children aged three to five

Typical three- to five-year-old children can . . .

Physical	At three, children are agile climbers, able to run well and pedal. They can use scissors, draw and paint and have an effective pincher grip. By five, they can climb stairs one foot per step, kick and throw a ball, hop and skip. They are skilful at climbing, swinging and sliding. They can copy actions shown on a screen and move to cues on dance mats or move in physical action games. As they develop fine motor control, children are able to use a computer mouse, scroll through pages and depress buttons (e.g. on a keyboard or control panel or mobile phone). The gradual coordination of movement in different planes or of both hands simultaneously makes using games consoles possible.
Cognitive	Three-year-old children can count by rote but have a limited grasp of quantities beyond two or three. They know that others see and hear things from a different perspective, but they have not yet developed cognitive perspective taking. Between three and five years old they start to be able to sort and match items and to arrange pictures or objects in order of size or time. They acquire concepts of more and less. By five, children have usually developed one-to-one correspondence when counting and can use categories such as size, shape and colour. They begin to be able to think about their own thinking and to understand that others have different thoughts. There are extensive opportunities to practise categorizing, matching, sorting and counting through computer games. As they become more able to think about routines and sequences, children are able to engage with menu choices, exploration and information gathering made possible through the internet.
Language	By age three, children talk in three- and four-word sentences, use personal pronouns, most prepositions and form plurals and can make themselves understood outside their homes. Between three and five years old they start to understand the use of symbols and know what many symbols in the environment signify. Five-year-old children can talk about the past and present, give connected accounts of events, tell long stories and recite rhymes. They enjoy jokes and riddles and listening to stories.

(continued)

Table 3.1 continued

Typical three- to five-year-old children can . . .

	Three- to five-year-old children can identify stop, start and replay signs, identify their favourite games from icons and manage the symbols on a remote control. By five, they can provide a commentary of an event to accompany photographs or video.
Social and emotional	Around the age of three, children can join in pretend play with others and enjoy playing with bricks, small world toys and joining or acting out domestic activities. Between three and five years old children become more able to control their behaviour, grow in independence, develop empathy and understand rules and fairness. Five-year-old children choose their own friends and act to protect younger children. They have a defined sense of humour. Turn taking and sharing is well developed and five-year-olds can cooperate with others. As they develop their social behaviour, children are able to follow rules for play set out in the design of the technology or by adults caring for them. They are able to take turns and offer help to each other (although their ability to explain how to do things still runs behind their ability to show what should be done). Children respond to animations and rewards for success which appeal to their sense of humour.

(2009: 1), we use 'competence' as an umbrella term to cover a complex of information, knowledge, skills, beliefs and values. These are generalized statements that are provided to give an indication of the kinds of things that children in this age range can do, but they are not intended to offer a yardstick for the development of any one child. The table describes development in four separate dimensions, but growing up encompasses all of these and any child's use of technology will be influenced by interactions between their physical, cognitive, language and social and emotional development. The first paragraph in each section outlines a broad range of characteristics of children aged three to five; the second paragraph indicates developing competences that relate to technology.

Just as children's learning can be in cognitive, social or emotional spheres, so too their homes and playrooms are cognitive, social and emotional environments. Playrooms are not just places where children go to learn about language or numbers or science. They are social settings where children acquire the ways of the preschool community and learn how to fit in by learning how to ask for something, how to make friends and how to relate to new adults. Emotional learning happens in the playroom, too. Individual children learn to control their own feelings of anger, find out what makes them happy or sad, articulate their own feelings and understand how others express their feelings. Children's homes are more evidently social and emotional environments, but cognitive learning also happens there. Understanding language, counting and quantity, time, symbols and the physical environment is nurtured through everyday family interactions and actions.

Yelland, Lee, O'Rourke and Harrison (2008) call for educators and practitioners to attend to what they describe as 'new learning'. The new forms of learning they identify include knowing how to make use of new technologies, learning to work collaboratively to solve problems in creative and innovative ways and knowing how to learn and how to access expertise and communicate ideas. This kind of learning is evident when children are able to listen to and comment on what others have said, contribute to brainstorming sessions and communicate graphically. Drawing on work by Kalantzis and Cope (2008), they argue that these new forms of learning which go beyond traditional, individually-focused learning are necessary if children are to acquire the ways of thinking and acting expected of them in the twenty-first century; this requires learning that goes beyond the reproduction of given ideas and information that is often prioritized in schools and is inherent in some closely prescribed curricula. Focusing on new learning means that rather than schools and teachers seeing their task as passing on a set of skills and knowledge which can be readily assessed, their role should be reconceptualized as being concerned with ways of communicating, thinking and working with others. New technologies are central to this concept of new learning, and they claim that 'young children are capable of understanding, making sense of and communicating concepts and ideas in multimodal ways and . . . can frequently incorporate the effective use of ICT to strengthen and amplify their learning' (Yelland *et al.* 2008: 146).

Theories of learning

Two major theories about how young children learn have influenced the thinking of educational practitioners, policy makers and researchers in the Western developed world. These ideas have shaped expectations and practice in early years settings and have influenced thinking about learning and appropriate educational or developmental experiences for young children. The first of these theories is that formulated by Piaget (e.g. 1926, 1932, 1954) and Piaget and Inhelder (1956). The second is sociocultural theory, which has its origins in the work of Russian psychologists, most notably Vygotsky. Piaget and Vygotsky were both born in 1896 and began publishing in the 1920s, but while Piaget lived until 1980, Vygotsky died in 1934. Piaget left an extensive body of writing, published in French and English from the 1920s onwards, while Vygotsky's ideas did not become well known outside Russia until they were published in English several decades later (e.g. Vygotsky 1962, 1978). Each of these theorists was influenced by a particular goal which shaped his endeavours to understand children's learning. Piaget began with an interest in epistemology, and he pursued this by examining how children acquire knowledge and adapt to the environment as they grow older. Vygotsky's work was shaped by his Marxist perspective. He was concerned with the forces which shape society and the role of social organization in the transmission of knowledge and skills to succeeding generations. In each case, their work has been developed and critiqued by other theorists and researchers and adopted by educators seeking ideas to underpin practice.

Piaget's theory: children's developing knowledge

Piaget adopts a developmental approach in his investigations and writing. He sets out to describe the ways of knowing about the world and thinking and acting in the world that characterize children from birth to adolescence, an approach which gave rise to Piaget's stage theory of development. Piaget focuses on children's mental processes: the ways in which children understand the world and how this understanding changes as children get older. He argues that development was driven by the interaction between the child and their environment, often characterized as positioning the child as a lone explorer actively constructing their world. He argues that children make sense of the world and objects in it through their existing mental structures, but the environment is also influential, driving learners to make changes in their cognitive processing as a result of new encounters with objects and experiences. If the child's current ways of understanding the world are sufficient to make satisfactory sense of the new information, it is assimilated into the existing mental structures and equilibrium is maintained. However, if the existing mental structures cannot make sense of new information or experiences then they are changed (through a process referred to as 'accommodation') to take account of the challenge, and a new equilibrium is reached. But these processes do not simply result in a gradual accumulation of knowledge or understanding. According to Piaget, children's ways of understanding and operating in the world can be categorized into four distinct stages. These stages move from making sense of the world through senses, then actions, to progressively more internalized manipulation of symbols and concepts until abstract, logical thought is reached.

Piaget's work has been subject to extensive criticism (e.g. Bower 1974, Bryant 1984, Donaldson 1978), particularly his linear, stepwise and unidirectional theory of developmental progress and his construction of children's thinking and learning as being initially immature, naive and limited in comparison with adult forms of thought. Researchers have shown that children are able to do much more than Piaget's original experiments suggest if they are engaged in more meaningful tasks, questions are posed differently or the testing equipment is designed differently. Later evidence also reveals that development proceeds in a more fluid and less unidirectional manner than Piaget suggests, and that children acquire new understandings in one area of development ahead of another or employ more or less sophisticated knowledge depending on the circumstances. Nevertheless, despite the extensive evidence modifying the original claims, Piaget's stage theory of development has a powerful and enduring influence on our conception of learning processes, the development of knowledge and the design of environments that support learning at different ages (Thomas 2007).

The legacy of Piaget's theory of learning and development persists in the ways in which children are grouped in early years settings, in the emphasis on children engaging in active exploration and in the focus on providing an environment and resources to stimulate learning. Preschool settings and schools in the UK group children by age rather than family-style mixed age groups, and provision for learning and ways of developing are then targeted at expectations that are considered typical for each stage. Resource-rich playrooms in which staff set out equipment and activities are a response to ideas about the child learning through personal, active exploration of the world. Some practitioners see their role mainly as a provider and observer, setting up the environment and then allowing children to explore and experiment freely while adults observe and record and then plan the next steps.

The debate about how technology should be used by young children reflects some of these ideas about the process of learning. Writers such as Healy (1998) argue that using computers is damaging for preschool children because it undermines developmental tasks. This argument rests on Piaget's claims that particular ways of learning are associated with defined ages, in a staged and normalized pattern of development. However, studies by developmental psychologists (e.g. Hughes 1986) indicate that development is not fixed in discrete stages, and evidence from neuroscience shows that although there are sensitive periods for sensory development, there is no suggestion of parallels in other areas of development (Blakemore and Frith 2005).

Other writers base their criticisms of the early use of technology on the screen-based nature of computers. These writers are concerned that this is a less effective medium for learning during the preschool years than engagement in active, physical manipulation of concrete objects. This seems likely to be another legacy of Piagetian thinking about developmental stages which has been over-taken by later studies, suggesting that children have various ways of knowing and responding that depend on the circumstances of the environment.

While we have pointed to challenges to Piaget's ideas, his work has provided important insights into children's development. He makes it clear that children do not know more because they receive more inputs over time, but rather that they actively construct their knowledge through the processes of assimilation and accommodation, and that they are driven to explore and make sense of the world. Children growing up with technology are curious and ready to both explore and try out what they already know. At home and in preschool, they incorporate new ways of engaging with technology that modify their existing understanding in a continuous spiral of sense making and growing competence. But while Piaget's work emphasizes the child's role as an explorer, sociocultural theory looks at the young learner in a broader social and cultural context.

Sociocultural approaches to learning

Sociocultural theory is the second of the key theories mentioned above and underpins the thinking about learning in this book. We are drawn to this way of thinking about learning because its central claim that children learn through dialogue and interactions with others makes sense, particularly in the early years. Adopting this perspective means being concerned with the influence of the contexts in which children learn, how learning varies with social and cultural experiences and the ways in which adults, other children, tools and resources support and shape learning. For Vygotsky, the most influential sociocultural theorist in educational thinking in the UK and elsewhere, the context in which children learn goes beyond the immediate setting of home or nursery to include the influence of history and the political and economic circumstances of the environment in which the learner lives. Schaffer (2004: 216) argues that his 'principal achievement was to have shown the gains to be made in our understanding when children are treated as part of the "social whole" and not detached from their environmental context'.

Vygotsky's work begins with the premise that children inherit the cultural tools of the society in which they live, and then goes on to study this process. By 'cultural tools' he means the ways of living in and making sense of the world that are shared by a society, ranging from technological resources such as clocks, cars, computers and cranes to ideas and concepts like mathematics, scientific theories and, most critically, language. Importantly for our research, technology is both a part of the context which influences children's learning outcomes and is one of the cultural tools which they make their own as they learn. Vygotsky argued that children acquire cultural tools through their interactions with the adults and older children that surround them, and use this inheritance to make sense of and act in their world.

Children learn how to use cultural tools whether their environment is explicitly educational or not, as adults or peers demonstrate the use of the cultural tools of their society. For example, we observed nursery staff show a girl how to use the viewfinder on a video camera. At home, that same child might have learnt how to send a photograph to her uncle on a mobile phone or rehearse her understanding of family relationships as she scrolled through digital photographs. Sociocultural theory sees learning as a cooperative venture: children's understandings become internalized and learning shifts from inter-personal (i.e. between individuals) to intrapersonal (i.e. within an individual) – from joint thinking to individual understanding – as they solve problems, tackle new endeavours and play with others (Schaffer 2004).

An important part of Vygotsky's theory of learning – and central to our concept of guided interaction described in Chapter 5 – is what is usually translated as the Zone of Proximal Development (ZPD), although it may be more helpfully thought of as the zone of potential development (Alexander 2000). The ZPD expresses the difference between what a child can achieve alone (e.g. reading a story, completing a jigsaw or using a digital camera) and what they can do with support from an adult or a child with more developed skills or understanding. To use the same examples, a child may be able to decode more of the text of a book, use colour and shape as well as picture clues to complete a puzzle or be introduced to the zoom function on the camera to capture a more detailed image if they have support from another person. Building on existing knowledge with help from others moves the child to new and more developed understanding and attainment – from potential development to actual development. As learners become able to accomplish actions or tasks independently, they shift from reliance on external assistance from another person to internal understanding and guidance.

Guided participation

Vygotsky is most concerned with explicit and didactic support for children's learning, but others suggest that the concept of the ZPD and all that it implies for support for children's learning is also relevant to less formal forms of instruction, such as social interactions with adults and peers at home and in the community. Rogoff (1990, 2003) demonstrates how parents, siblings and members of the wider community support learning, describing this support as guided participation and drawing attention to the way in which the help of others allows children to take part in the social life of their family and society in ways which they could not achieve alone. Rogoff suggests that there are two key forms of guided participation: mutual bridging of meanings and mutual structuring of opportunities. Mutual bridging of meanings refers to the way in which the adult and child participants in any activity have to adjust their perspective as they work together to accomplish something. This bridging might be nonverbal or verbal: Rogoff, Mistry, Göncü and Mosier (1993) give the example of a baby exploring whether or not playdough was edible by holding a small piece of dough to his mouth and looking questioningly at his mother. Alternatively, a caregiver can pick up a verbal comment from a child and ask questions to explore the child's intent or suggest alternatives. Mutual structuring of participation happens as children observe or take part in the routines and events of everyday life in their society. Typically, children at home have more opportunities to observe and learn to participate in the adult world than they do in the separate environment of the playroom, with its focus on child-oriented provision. While the playroom offers advantages in terms of resources that can be used independently by young learners, peers with whom to practise the negotiation of mutual meaning and time and space to pursue individual interests, the activities in this child-oriented world often lack the engaging power of authenticity (Stephen, Cope, Oberski and Shand 2008).

Both mutual bridging of meanings and mutual structuring of participation are enacted in culturally-specific and appropriate ways. The norms of their family and community and the child's own interests shape the actions, chores, play, conversations and routines in which they are able to participate and the things they learn to do competently. Brooker (2002) has demonstrated how children growing up in homes that are culturally different from the majority population have opportunities to participate in varying aspects of everyday life and will arrive at nursery or school with different competences and expectations. In one of the Bangladeshi families taking part in Brooker's study, a little girl had learnt to chop onions expertly using a heavy knife, while children in the Anglo families were more often kept out of the kitchen because their mothers were anxious about danger or breakages. In one of the disadvantaged Anglo families, the youngest girl's favourite activities at home were playing with playdough, paint, Lego and bricks – all experiences that were familiar when she encountered them in the classroom. Play at home in the Bangladeshi families was less structured or resourced by adults; children were generally expected to be more self-reliant, perhaps watching television or playing with small world figures or with other children, and this could mean that these children had less experience of participating in the kinds of activities with which they were asked to engage when they started school.

Interaction

For those who adopt a sociocultural approach, dialogue and interaction are at the heart of the acting and thinking with others that drives learning. Referring to the implications of Vygotsky's ideas about learning, Alexander argues that

> While it is clear that this approach challenges the once popular view of the teacher as a hands-off 'facilitator', it is important to stress that it does not herald a return to the traditional model of teaching as mere telling or transmitting. Where both of the earlier models implied activity on one side of the teacher–pupil relationship but passivity on the other – active pupils and passive teachers in one, passive pupils and active teachers in the other – the new approach demands both pupil engagement *and* teacher intervention. And the principal means by which pupils actively engage and teachers constructively intervene is through talk.
>
> (Alexander 2004: 12, original emphasis)

Alexander is concerned here with children of primary school age. Our findings suggest that for preschool children, support for learning needs to go beyond talk, although that is not to diminish the value of adults and children talking together in playrooms. In their exploration of the practices that could be observed in the preschool centres that were most effective in adding value to children's developmental progress, Siraj-Blatchford and Sylva (2004) find that it was the degree of sustained shared thinking, when children and adults engaged in dialogue that involved cognitive challenge and construction, that made a difference.

Later developments of sociocultural theory make it clear that learning is not a one-way process: children do not merely absorb what others demonstrate to them, but contribute actively to society's understanding and knowledge. Corsaro (1997: 18) argues that children do not just adopt and internalize what is given, but reinvent and reproduce as they 'negotiate, share and create culture with adults and each other'. He terms this 'interpretative reproduction' in order to draw attention to the way in which children 'are not simply internalizing society and culture, but are actively *contributing to cultural production and change*' (original emphasis). Technology offers many opportunities for and examples of this process of cultural production by children and young people. In their imaginative play, children make technology work for them, or use props to stand in for technology to which they do not have access.

Scaffolding (Wood, Bruner and Ross 1976) occurs when adult actions and talk structure the child's actions or the nature of the task in a way that supports successful completion and learning. In Chapter 5 we look at the ways in which researchers have explored the kinds of help for children's learning that occur in different circumstances and consider scaffolding in more detail. In the next section of this chapter we draw attention to the implications for preschool practice that follow from a socioculturally-informed pedagogy. This means taking account of what the children know or can do alone, and then going on to find ways of assisting them to move beyond this. This approach focuses attention on the need for adults to support learning in ways that guide children to participate with increasing competence and independence, at home or in the nursery setting. We describe why we think this is particularly important for learning with technology, especially computers.

Pedagogy

The interactions that support learning can be spontaneous and intuitive, just part of the accepted social practice of parenting or child–adult relationships. In other circumstances, particularly in preschool education, there is a need to think about and plan for the kind of support that will most effectively enhance children's learning (i.e. to develop a planned and purposeful pedagogy). Pedagogy can be defined as all the actions and intentions of practitioners that make a difference to children's learning. It can include interacting with children through teaching, modelling, prompting or questioning to nurture developmental change, learning or the acquisition of specific skills. At home, pedagogical interactions are often implicit and taken for granted, such as when a parent helps a child to get dressed or a sibling shows a younger brother or sister how to move up a level on a games console. There are other times when parents set out to provide experiences and engage in dialogue that is planned explicitly to help children learn how to do something: this might be crossing the road or finding out about something (e.g tropical fish or motor sport) so that they can share in a family interest. Pedagogy can be implicit in preschool settings, too. Practitioners implicitly model desirable ways of interacting with others as they eat a meal with the children or intuitively know when to hold out a hand to a child learning to walk on a balance beam. Other forms of learning are more explicitly planned and attended to: healthy eating is introduced to children through talk at snack time or when food is being prepared, displays of nutritious food are planned and games are designed to help children identify healthy and unhealthy foods.

As well as being achieved explicitly or implicitly, pedagogy can involve distal and proximal actions. Distal actions are those carried out by adults when children are not present, as happens when practitioners reflect on their observations and plan next steps in learning for individuals for the coming week. Proximal actions take place during direct interactions with the child, such as drawing attention to a piece of a jigsaw puzzle or prompting some 'what if' thinking. We return to these distal and proximal forms of pedagogy when we discuss guided interaction in playrooms and at home.

Whether the support for learning that adults offer is informal and intuitive or part of a planned pedagogy, it has to begin with intersubjectivity. It is this process of sharing 'knowing' between adults and children that makes dialogue and support for learning possible. Practitioners need to tune in to children's perspectives and understanding through talk and observation of what children can do themselves before they can begin to find appropriate ways to support them to do what they cannot yet manage independently. But children need to be partners in this relationship, ready to engage with the adult perspective and talk about their understandings or skills or put them into operation.

As well as establishing and continuing to be concerned with intersubjectivity, a sociocultural approach makes other demands of practitioners. Bruner (1996, Chapter 2) argues that practitioners have to see children as knowledgeable. He sets out four ways of thinking about young learners:

- as learning through imitation or copying a model;
- as learning through instruction, in which knowledge is transmitted from adult to child;
- as learning through thinking, shaped by dialogue with adults;
- as knowledgeable, but in need of support to understand and to bridge the gap between personal and shared or cultural knowledge.

The first three perspectives influence the pedagogical actions through which practitioners attempt to support learning, although in preschool settings in the UK, USA and Europe, there is typically little effort to support learning through direct instruction. The fourth perspective is more challenging as it requires practitioners to find ways of understanding how the child sees the world and to help young learners to distinguish between their personal knowledge or theories and the explanations and theories that are commonly accepted in their community. This could involve finding out how a child makes sense of the way a zoom lens works and introducing them to the similarities and differences between their understanding and commonly held explanations. Or, in the social sphere, it could involve finding out how a preschooler constructs the impact of their behaviour on others and introducing them to alternative perspectives and ideas about what is desirable. Whatever the specific example, the essence of this way of seeing young learners is as sense-makers who have developed their own way of knowing the world through their experiences in it.

If we take seriously the understanding that children gain through supportive interactions with others and their own sense making, we will see learning happening wherever children are and not just in nurseries, playgroups or classrooms formally designated as spaces for education. Learning happens at home, in the street, with friends and with the extended family. However, as Tizard and Hughes (1984) demonstrate so effectively, home and nursery are very different environments, with different potentials and opportunities to support children's learning. They argue that children are able to be powerful learners at home because they are supported by shared understandings with their parents and siblings, sensitive one-to-one interactions and authentic experiences. We discuss the ways in which this played out in our studies in later chapters. Preschool settings can offer a greater range of possibilities for social learning, experiences and activities that are not available at home, as well as opportunities to employ decontextualized or transferable knowledge and understanding. However, managing the needs of a group of children means that practitioners may not be able to offer the support of a responsive and attentive adult as readily as parents can at home. It is difficult for practitioners who are with children for limited periods of time to appreciate what a child can do and express when they are in the familiar emotional and social environment of home, yet it is these conditions that make the most of learning opportunities.

Not only do the structural circumstances of home and preschool or school differ, but the children and adults begin with what Gonzalez, Moll and Amanti (2005) refer to as different 'funds of knowledge'. The challenge for preschool practitioners is to be able to recognize the existing understandings and skills that children have developed in their lives at home and in the community, and create opportunities for them to add to this knowledge and practise their skills in new contexts. This is a process of mediation that is an integral part of the practitioner's role. Effective support for learning involves recognizing the kind of opportunities the learner needs next, arranging the environment to offer these opportunities in an engaging and positive way and supplying the resources that will help, while avoiding those that will hinder. Practitioners also act as mediators as they interact directly with children, conveying pleasure or fun, minimizing frustration and sharing interests.

Play, technology and learning

Technology, as well as adults and peers, can support and mediate learning, and the technologies encountered will afford or prompt learning in different modes. Just as climbing frames and slides invite different forms of movement, technological resources shape response modes and ways of interacting: cameras focus attention on visual communication, mobile phones offer text and spoken ways of communicating and computer games require interaction by keyboard or mouse to respond to textual, auditory or visual stimuli. Yelland *et al.* (2008) argue that the multimodal forms of expression and communication that technologies now offer are a significant change in our culture, and one which primary schools with their traditional focus on text and print can find challenging. Children who have developed a preference for, or particular competence with, visual or spatial forms of expression that have been facilitated by technology in the preschool context can find that these forms of expression are considered less valuable than competence with text and print in school. The studies we describe in this book make it clear that the funds of knowledge about technology that children acquire at home, and the ways of communicating or demonstrating that knowledge, differ from the privileged knowledge they encounter in educational settings.

Children's behaviour is often described as play, and this play might involve imaginary worlds in which children act out features of everyday life, such as driving a car, working in a shop or being a parent. Play is notoriously difficult to define (Sutton-Smith 1997), and the many different ways of categorizing play (e.g. cooperative, solitary, physical, manipulative, imaginary, creative, etc.) are testimony to the range of behaviour thought of as play. Indeed, our observations of children talking on a mobile phone or using a remote control prompt questions about the extent to which these activities can be classed as play, given that they use them in exactly the same way as adults, and the behaviours that both parents and practitioners describe as 'playing on the computer' can only sometimes be described as playful (Plowman and Stephen 2005).

Play is usually thought of as characterized by spontaneity, being of intrinsic interest rather than for external reward and having no prescribed outcomes. Play offers opportunities for rehearsal and mastery, for trying things out, for taking risks and for concentrating on the process with minimum concern for the outcome. But play can also be repetitive and stereotypical and lack the cognitive challenge that sociocultural theory suggests is necessary to provide the impetus for new ways of understanding or to acquire new skills or tools to make sense of the world.

Play has a cherished place in preschool provision and practice, and it is considered by many to be the defining feature of the early years environment. For many parents, too, play is just what children do, a natural process that occurs without adult intervention and both entertains and educates. For policy makers, play is seen as making a powerful contribution to children's learning.

Scottish policy refers to taking advantage of the opportunities for learning presented by 'spontaneous play' and 'planned, purposeful play' (Scottish Executive 2007). The *Framework for Children's Learning for 3 to 7-year-olds in Wales* (Welsh Assembly Government 2008: 6) refers to play as a 'serious business', important for social development and fundamental to intellectual development.

Despite these claims, play is an under-researched and undertheorized phenomenon and its contribution to learning is not clearly understood. There are clear theoretical arguments for the contribution that play can make to learning in the work of Vygotsky, but, as Bodrova (2008) has pointed out recently, this is not any kind of play, but play that meets specific criteria: children create an imaginary situation, take on and act out roles and follow a set of rules determined by those roles. In their review of the literature, the early years special interest group of the British Educational Research Association (BERA-SIG 2003) set out a number of untested assumptions about play and critiqued the ways in which thinking about the relationship between play and learning has become muddled with ideas about child-centred and progressive pedagogies that also emphasize exploration, experiential learning and choice or free play. They conclude that 'research evidence for the efficacy of play is mixed and, in some areas, problematic' and that playing is not a sufficient condition for learning to occur: adults (either parents or practitioners) need to ensure that the conditions support learning through play. Siraj-Blatchford and Sylva (2004) found that it was when play involved cognitive challenge and engagement in 'potentially instructive play activities' that it made a difference to the effectiveness with which preschool settings supported children's learning. Research suggests that when play is expected to be a medium for learning, whether the play is technological or carried out with traditional toys, it is the responsibility of adults to ensure that the conditions in which the children are invited to play support learning.

Just as there can be no expectations that all play supports learning, we must acknowledge that individual children enjoy different kinds of play. In studies of children's feelings about their preschool settings and early primary classes we have found that they are discriminating participants with distinct preferences for particular kinds of play and activities. Preschool settings must offer a wide range of play opportunities if they are to satisfy the preferences of all the children attending (Stephen 2003). We discuss children's preferences among the technologies that they grow up with at home in Chapter 6, but it is important to note here that children make individual choices about the resources with which they want to play that are not necessarily the same as the choices of their families (Stephen, McPake, Plowman and Berch-Heyman 2008). When we asked children what they liked to do and what engaged them in the first year of primary school, their answers were dominated by activities that they described as playing. These activities were characterized by an element of choice, opportunities to have some control over time and space, a lack of predetermined or correct outcomes and a degree of authenticity, or at least an obvious link to authentic experiences (Stephen, Cope, Oberski and Shand 2008). Although preschool practitioners talk about children playing with the computer, we found that some computer activities for three- to five-year-olds olds invite exploration and playfulness, but many others are designed to attract children to practise new skills and are restrictive in the responses they invite. If children are to become engaged in play that supports learning, with or without technology, then not only do educators need to pay attention to the kind of play opportunities offered, but they also need to take account of the preferences and expectations of the young learners.

Children's competences, responsive adults

Young children are active participants in the learning process, making sense of their experiences in terms of what they already know and modifying their understanding as they encounter new ideas and experiences. The critical role of the social environment in which they are learning is made clear in the sociocultural perspective on the learning process, particularly the importance of an adult who can support a child to achieve what they cannot yet do alone. The social and relational aspects of the learning process mean that interactions, scaffolding and the mediation of other people and resources make important contributions to learning. In later chapters we discuss how adults at home and in preschool settings can support children's learning about and through the technologies they encounter as they grow up. For families this support is often informal and implicit, but the pedagogy of practitioners in educational settings is more likely to include explicit plans for actions and interactions.

Summarizing their findings from a substantial review of research into the way two- to five-year-old children learn, Bowman, Donovan and Burns (2000) point to two critical features of the learning process: that young children are competent and active participants, but they nevertheless benefit from the sensitive support of adults.

> [T]he striking feature of modern research is that it describes unexpected competencies in young children . . . These data focus attention on the child's exposure to learning opportunities, calling into question simplistic conceptualizations of developmentally appropriate practice that do not recognize the newly understood competencies of very young children, and they highlight the importance of individual differences in children, their past experiences and their present contexts . . . Research from a variety of theoretical perspectives suggests that a defining feature of a supportive environment is a responsible and responsive adult.
>
> (Bowman *et al.* 2000: 5)

The research and theory we have examined in this chapter make it clear that if children's learning is to be promoted in preschool settings, it is essential that the environment in which they spend their time is designed to offer sensitive support for learning. This entails not only the recognition of children's existing competences, but also the actions and interactions that extend the child's learning from what they can do unaided to new ways of being that allow them to participate in and adapt to the ways of their culture.

Chapter 4

Curriculum, pedagogy and technology in preschool

The educational experiences offered to young children in preschool settings reflect the decisions made by policy makers, providers and practitioners about the curriculum to be followed and the pedagogical approaches which will support children's learning and achieve the intended outcomes. The decisions about what these experiences should be are influenced by ideas that society in general and those who work in each setting hold about children, childhood and learning. For example, practice in the UK is concerned with encouraging children to become independent learners, but in societies that are influenced by the Confucian tradition, such as Korea, the focus is on whole-class teaching and the authority of the teacher (Kwon 2003). In contrast, preschool education in Norway is thought of as promoting traditional ideas about a 'good Norwegian childhood' as well as being a tool with which to develop the welfare state (Strand 2006).

In Chapter 3 we described how ideas from Piaget's stage theory of development still shape practice in preschool settings. Other aspects of provision for young children reflect the ideas of pioneers of nursery provision, such as Margaret McMillan, who focused on health and physical and sensory development, or Susan Issacs, who advocated free play as a means for children to learn about the world and cope with powerful emotions such as fear and anxiety.

There can be a tension between those who see early childhood as a time of innocence that is to be protected and those who construct children as competent and able to make sense of and learn from many experiences; the contrast between these perspectives is clearly evident in the different positions taken about the appropriateness of digital technologies for young children described in Chapter 2. Social, economic and political ideas and expectations also shape decisions about the purpose and outcomes of early years provision. In Scotland and England early years education is expected to contribute to the development of individuals, but it is also expected to work for the greater benefit of society as children grow into economically active citizens. Governments also see early intervention and childcare as ways of helping to break cycles of deprivation and poverty and reduce social and economic burdens on society. The *Early Years Framework* (Scottish Government 2008a) is clear that services for young children and their families are expected to reduce the costs of failure and that improvements in early years experiences are a central element of their strategy for 'regenerating communities, reducing crime, tackling substance misuse and improving employability'. Early years education is also expected to shape children's adoption of society's values and morals. For instance, in Sweden the early years curriculum aims to support children's participation in democratic life, while in Japan the celebration of national days is used to structure educational experiences and develop appreciation of the national culture.

The early years curriculum

Despite the potential for variation across societies, Bertram and Pascal (2002) find a number of common features in the curricular guidance for preschool children over three years of age in the 20 mostly, but not exclusively, developed nations they survey.

- The curriculum is structured around areas of learning rather than traditional subjects and the emphasis is on a holistic approach.
- Six areas of development are at the core of the different curricula: social and emotional; cultural, aesthetic and creative; physical; environmental; language and literacy; and numeracy.
- The focus is on an active, play-based curriculum which aims to support children to become independent learners.
- The practitioner is usually thought of as supporting and facilitating development and learning rather than as a teacher or instructor who leads or directs learning through a more didactic approach.

These features are common to the distinct curricula developed by each of the four national education systems of the UK. The areas of development may be differently labelled and grouped, but school subjects such as history and mathematics are avoided everywhere. The emphasis is on the whole child, play as a medium for learning, experiential learning and the crucial role of adults as supporters of learning.

The guidance for practice developed by the National Association for the Education of Young Children (NAEYC 2009) underpins the pedagogical approach adopted in the USA known as 'developmentally appropriate practice', and it also represents the consensus on pedagogy in the UK (Siraj-Blatchford 1999). Settings that adopt this approach aim to ensure:

- Children experience a balance between self-initiated activity and practitioner-guided opportunities for learning.
- Meaningful choices between activities are available.
- There is scope for exploration.

- Children spend their time in a mix of independent, small-group and whole-group activities.
- Play is an important – but not the only – medium for learning.
- Practitioners pose questions, demonstrate actions, suggest alternatives and model problem solving and reflection.
- Learning and behavioural development is observed and recorded.

While there will be gaps between the espoused curriculum and everyday practice in some cases (Dunn and Kontos 1997), typically children in the UK can expect their preschool playrooms to offer a range of activities and learning opportunities to support their social, emotional, physical, aesthetic and cognitive development. They will be able to spend much of a session choosing freely between the options arranged by staff to allow independent use; they will also spend some time each day involved with a small group of peers in activities selected by a practitioner who knows them well and some time with a larger group of children for singing or story time. The practitioners who care for the children and support their learning recognize that there are expectations that the provision they offer will result in children achieving planned outcomes. However, they see themselves in a more nurturing role, responding to children's evolving interests and maintaining an environment in which children can develop in individual ways (Stephen and Brown 2004).

ICT in early years settings

Across the developed world the growth of interest in ICT as an educational tool has extended from school provision to early years settings, although the presence of technology in the playroom and the extent to which it features in the curriculum varies from one country to another. Nevertheless, there appears to be a widespread desire to prepare children for a technological world. In their review of the literature about preschool curriculum and pedagogy in the USA, Bowman, Donovan and Burns (2000: 228) devote a section to the implications of the learning of young children using computers. They conclude that across several subject matter areas, computers can positively affect how children learn and think, as well as their metacognitive skills, but they argue against technology as a substitute for hands-on experiences. Combining computer activities with appropriate non-technological activities gives the greatest benefit, they say. They qualify this with a warning that 'integrating technology into the curriculum demands effort, time and commitment'. The evidence they review leads them to conclude that the software used should have educational goals that match those of the practitioners and that multimedia capabilities, such as music, animation and interactivity, must be consistent with the practitioners' intended learning purposes if they are to contribute positively to children's learning.

The Swedish preschool curriculum draws attention to the need to give all children access to computers in order to promote the ideals of equity, justice and democracy (Ljung-Djärf, Åberg-Bengtsson and Ottosson 2005), and technical equipment and staff training have been provided to ensure that children engage with computers in particular. In Norway, the framework which sets out the expectations for the curriculum and pedagogy for kindergartens reflects the traditional Norwegian emphasis on nature and the environment, but refers to children learning about how technology can be used in play and everyday life. It also suggests that staff should build on and extend children's experiences of technological toys and the technology they experience around them.

Technology has become part of the learning environment of most preschool settings in the UK, and each of the four national curricula refers to ICT as providing a valuable learning opportunity for young children. The Foundation Stage in Wales, for children from three to seven years old, seeks to ensure that children can make use of ICT, such as interactive books and audiotapes, to express their imagination and creativity and to develop language, literacy and communication skills in several areas of the curriculum. Similarly, in Northern Ireland the expectation is that children from four years old will have access to a wide range of reading materials, including screen-based text and a variety of computer packages to support their mathematical development.

Practice guidance for the Early Years Foundation in England, for children up to five years old, includes a specific section on ICT, listing the development expected from birth to 60 months, along with notes about supportive practice and planning and appropriate resources. For instance, at 16 to 26 months practitioners are urged to include technological resources in play choices and children are expected to be interested in pressing buttons and learning how to operate simple toys or equipment. Between 40 and 60 months the expectation is that children will be able to work through a simple program on a computer, use a mouse and keyboard, play with programmable toys and use ICT for familiar functions such as selecting a telephone number or changing the television channel.

In Scotland, where our studies were conducted, *A Curriculum Framework for Children 3 to 5,* the first formalized curriculum guidance for young learners, makes little mention of ICT, but does refer to technology as an important aspect of the environment:

> As children use blocks, put on a warm jumper, look through a magnifying glass, clamber on to a climbing frame, use a computer or travel by train, they become aware of the everyday uses of technology in the home, in transport, in communication and in leisure.
>
> (Scottish Consultative Council on the Curriculum 1999: 23)

In 2003 the policy decision to promote the use of ICT in early years settings in the public, private and voluntary sectors in Scotland resulted in

Early Learning, Forward Thinking, a new strategy and curriculum guidance (Learning and Teaching Scotland 2003). This was the only amendment to the curriculum guidance in Scotland for a period of about ten years, an indication of the importance that policy makers have come to attach to ICT as a tool for learning. The process of developing the guidance and implementation strategy began with a review of the research literature about young children using ICT (Stephen and Plowman 2002), supplemented by *'Come back in two years!'*, the observational study referred to in Chapter 1 that gave a snapshot description of existing practice (Stephen and Plowman 2003a).

In *'Come back in two years!'* we draw a distinction between developing familiarity with the technology (i.e. learning *about* technology) – 'The whole world is technology and therefore they have to get used to it . . .' (Pam, nursery school) – and offering learning opportunities across the curriculum areas (i.e. using technology as a tool to learn *with* and *through*):

> The social skills, their maths skills and their hand–eye co-ordination and fine motor skills have developed really quickly. We do a lot of rhyming words and it's easy for them to get the concept of that when it's visual as well.
>
> (Rena, nursery school)

> Every area of the curriculum you can cover if you look to cover it.
>
> (Jo, private sector nursery)

Early Learning, Forward Thinking (Learning and Teaching Scotland 2003: 3) emphasizes that 'Learning with ICT can provide added value in extending learning opportunities for children, often in ways that only an ICT resource can offer. Such encounters can take place in all areas of the curriculum'. The guidance draws on this distinction between learning about, with and through technology to stress the need to develop appropriate pedagogy and to make the most effective use of resources. Practitioners are urged to draw on their in-depth knowledge of individual children to support their interactions with technology and to acknowledge each child's feelings about engaging with ICT and to model reflection and exploration when using such resources. There is an explicit warning to not let the technology drive events in playrooms, but to make it part of existing and evolving good pedagogical practice.

In the *Curriculum for Excellence*, a single curriculum framework which spans learners from three to 18 years old, the need to develop expertise with technologies receives explicit attention:

> Being skilled in using ICT is essential if children and young people are to be effective contributors, and to communicate and interact on a global scale . . . It is essential that all [practitioners] have opportunities to apply, reinforce and extend ICT skills within and across curriculum areas to help

equip children and young people with the learning and employability skills required for the twenty-first century.

(Learning and Teaching Scotland 2009a)

The experiences and outcomes for technologies that are set out for the Early Level (for children who are three to six years old) of the *Curriculum for Excellence* are summarized below:

- I enjoy playing with and exploring technologies to discover what they can do and how they can help us.
- I enjoy exploring and using technologies to communicate with others within and beyond my place of learning.
- I enjoy taking photographs or recording sound and images to represent my experiences and the world around me.
- I explore software and use what I learn to solve problems and present my ideas, thoughts or information.
- I am developing problem solving strategies, navigation and co-ordination skills, as I play and learn with electronic games, remote control or programmable toys.

(adapted from Learning and Teaching Scotland 2009b: 2–6)

Technology and resources in the playroom

Each of the seven settings in our initial observation study had at least one computer in the playroom with one exception, where the decision had been made to place it in a separate room. Only one setting had purchased any laptop computers, but these were offered to parents and children for use at home as part of a lending scheme rather than for use in the playroom. While laptops remain the exception in preschool settings, the case-study settings which took part in our subsequent research project entitled 'Interplay' (see Appendix 1) generally had several desktop computers as standard playroom equipment. Set on low tables with several chairs placed alongside, these were resources that children frequently went to during free play periods, and in some cases practitioners pre-loaded software to target a particular learning goal such as identifying rhyming words or initial letter sounds or working with mathematical concepts such as matching shapes. On other occasions children were encouraged to make a selection from alternative programmes by identifying icons on the screen and then choosing from the menu within a programme.

In 2003, we found only a few examples of children and practitioners using the internet together. In one setting the internet was used to help children to find out about dinosaurs and to follow an interest in snakes that developed as they built a model volcano. Elsewhere photographs of birds were downloaded for a display. At one private all-day setting, parents were invited to send emails to their child during the day and children were helped to respond. However, these instances of internet use in the playroom were not common; practitioners were much more likely to use the internet for administration and communication with colleagues. By 2009, many nurseries have their own website, but the use of the internet in the playroom remains limited. A look at the examples of good practice being highlighted on a national website designed to promote professional development in ICT reveals 11 projects, but none focus on internet use; there is much more attention on the site to the educational potential of cameras for photographs or movies (Learning and Teaching Scotland 2009c). The lack of internet connections in many of the playrooms and concerns about online safety explain why the web is not more widely used as a resource. A further limitation arises from the practitioners' views that they should only use resources that are clearly within the recognized educational canon. Even if it is possible to access the internet from a playroom, computer staff are generally uncomfortable about children logging on to the Barbie, Bratz, Club Penguin or Disney sites.

Over time, the range of ICT resources in preschool settings has widened as practitioners have become increasingly interested in the potential of the resources, as well as in their own ability to use them. Purchasing new technology is a regular feature of budget planning, sometimes explicitly encouraged by local authority and central government finance. In the course of Interplay, purchases included easier-to-handle digital video cameras and electronic microscopes, digital projectors and large screens for group work, electronic keyboards and other musical instruments and software designed to manipulate images, produce booklets or monitor individual children's use of and progress with specific packages.

Television and video players were widely available in the settings taking part in Interplay, but they were rarely integrated into playroom activities. Although audio equipment was frequently used to play music and sometimes to listen to stories, there was little use of these resources for recording children's voices, and practitioners at several settings identified the listening centre, a cassette or CD player with headphones, as a long-established but underused resource which they wanted to develop further during the course of the project. Practitioners talked enthusiastically about digital cameras, valuing the opportunity for immediate viewing of images that they offer. These resources were accessible for practitioners and children and appeared to act as an entry-level technology for inexperienced staff. We found cameras being used to take photographs for displays, to share special events or achievements with parents and to keep records of children's progress:

> They are instant and the children can use them as well . . . We use the digital camera in our observations of the children so that if they have an achievement like they climb to the top of the climbing frame for the very first time on their own then we can get a photograph of that immediately

and we can print it off immediately and then we can use that to write in their starting points that they have achieved this activity. And also it gives us something to show the parents when they come to pick them up: 'Look what your child has done today, this is the very first time they have done this.' So it gives an opportunity to build their self-esteem.

(Val, playgroup practitioner)

It's made me realize how many things are ICT that we didn't realize are ICT.

(Nuala, nursery teacher)

While digital still and video cameras offer considerable advantages in terms of immediacy and future use of images, they were seen as costly, not only for the initial purchase but also for printing and batteries. Similar cost issues were reported for computers as staff needed to find money in their budgets for printing costs, particularly when children were enthusiastic users of art and drawing programmes. Staff also mentioned other practical drawbacks, including the facts that cameras were too heavy for young children and headphones were too large. Some software was not responsive to children's needs or was built on inappropriate linguistic or cognitive expectations; for instance, in a rhyming game, the link between the visual prompt (a small tree) and the rhyming word ('rub a dub dub') was not appropriate for the children's vocabulary. To proceed in the game, the children needed to identify the illustration as a 'shrub'. Unable to do so, they lost interest and walked away from the computer.

Difficulties with finding appropriate locations in the playroom and ways of safeguarding technology which practitioners, at least initially, conceived of as expensive and vulnerable, were also raised. But with experience these concerns diminished and new routines evolved in the settings:

I encouraged children to use the listening centre independently, which they were so able to do . . . You know, we totally underestimate these children and I think we try too hard to protect our equipment'.

(Isobel, nursery class practitioner).

Despite the increasingly widespread use of digital cameras and other technologies in the playroom, we were struck by the dominance of computers in any conversations about ICT with practitioners and policy makers. Although they recognized that keyboards, mobile phones and digital cameras were part of the children's everyday lives in nursery and at home, it was clear that when it came to using ICT to support learning, it was traditional desktop computers that were the focus of attention. But screen-based desktop computers are not necessarily the most appropriate technology for young children. They were designed for individual adults to use in the workplace and are not suited to very young children because of their size, position and fixed location. Equipment produced for adults often has inappropriate physical and cognitive ergonomics for young children, yet young children are expected to adapt to products that have not been designed with them in mind. Preschool users are not scaled-down adults, so scaling down the hardware does not meet their specific requirements, which include ease of use, robustness and mobility. The usual reliance on text for input and output and the demand for fine motor control to use the mouse effectively means that standard desktop computers are ill suited to children who cannot yet read and are still developing the necessary dexterity.

There are growing numbers of products designed for use by younger children which avoid the use of a visual display, keyboard or mouse as the interface (Antle 2009; Eagle, Manches, O'Malley, Plowman and Sutherland 2008). Laptops do not need cables and so are more portable. Other products range from soft toys that communicate with the computer by radio transmitter to animatronic dogs and horses. Interactive books such as LeapPads are picture- and text-based and freestanding like traditional books, but children can hear the story and interact with sounds and pictures by using a stylus. Similar technologies may be more fun, better suited for moving around the playroom, easier to use collaboratively with peers and easier to integrate into children's play.

However, the design of these products is likely to be driven by the home market rather than the educational market, so the software may not necessarily have been designed to take account of pedagogic principles. Practitioners taking part in Interplay had doubts about whether technological toys (or toys that simulate technology, like toy laptops) offer valuable learning opportunities. In order to be confident about what a toy or software package has to offer, practitioners need to know if the model of learning and teaching inherent in the technology matches their preferred practice and fits with the pedagogical strategies used to support the children in their playrooms. It may be necessary to try out resources and software to discover both the advantages and disadvantages in the design features and pedagogical underpinnings. All design has a model of the teaching and learning process implicit in it, manifested by how the learner is conceptualized, how information is presented, whether or not and how learning is assessed and how feedback is used. Unfortunately, this model is rarely made explicit and staff do not have time to evaluate products in detail.

Integrating technologies into the learning environment

In a study of 11 preschool settings in the USA, Cuban (2001) finds that most kindergarten teachers offered computer activities as a free choice activity. The children were neither obliged to use the computer, nor obliged to produce any particular piece of work there. He concludes that the computer became another 'centre' in the playroom, incorporated into the existing practice rather than revolutionizing it. This incorporation, as opposed to a radical shift, is typical of the way in which the staff that participated in our studies reacted to the arrival of new technological resources. Generally, technologies were introduced into playrooms as a new resource to be added to existing provision (e.g. adding an electronic keyboard to the musical instruments) or as an alternative tool (e.g. using a camera to record a child's achievement rather than jotting it down on a sticky note to add to the profile). In some cases technology was used to add a different medium or stimulate children's interest and imagination. For example, in one of the Interplay settings the listening centre and puppet theatre were set out so they complemented each other, offering new stories to act out and props to encourage the retelling of stories heard on tape. Elsewhere, extracts of recorded music were used to stimulate children's reflection on mood and emotions and as a stimulus to movement.

Labbo, Sprague, Montero and Font (2000: 5) examine the ways in which teachers used the technology to meet children's learning needs. They outline three kinds of engagement in which it could be used effectively:

- brief targeted moments when adult and child worked together;
- spur-of-the-moment activities that arose from play or conversation;
- thematically linked activities, planned to present key concepts in a variety of ways.

But practitioners in Interplay often talked about the difficulty of finding time in a busy playroom to support an individual's encounters with ICT. Implicit in their concern was the recognition that these resources were not ones which they could necessarily expect children to use unaided: operational features of the technology may require the assistance of others, questions from practitioners can prompt exploration and problem solving and those who are hesitant may need the comfort of a familiar adult alongside.

> They use the video camera now and they use the dictaphone and they've got the metal detector and they've got all the science equipment, they've got walkie-talkies and all that sort of thing, so they are more confident. When we first put all the science and technology stuff out it lay in the corner and they just all stood and looked at it because they didn't know, and it took one of us to go and sit with them. But now – they would go and pick up all the things and the remote control cars and everything and use them properly.
>
> (Beth, nursery class practitioner)

Of course interactions with technology are not the only form of learning encounters that benefit from the presence of a more competent other. Sociocultural theories of learning, such as those of Vygotsky and Rogoff discussed in Chapter 3, point to the essential contribution made by adults. They help children to overcome physical barriers, suggest ways of thinking about problems, break tasks into manageable parts and facilitate participation in activities children could not do alone. The contribution that can be made by a responsive adult is evident when we see children who cannot yet read looking at books with a practitioner to find information, children getting help with building a sandcastle or children benefiting from suggestions about how to complete a seriation puzzle. Regardless of the kinds of technology available in a nursery, the most valuable resource for any child is the practitioner who cares for them, knows what interests them, understands what they can do alone and with help and interacts with them in a responsive manner. Perhaps because of their diverse education and training routes or the legacy of low status associated with childcare and the historically poor record of continuing professional development, preschool practitioners often doubt their competence. This is particularly the case with innovations such as engaging children in learning with ICT or using ICT to enhance practice. The practitioners with whom we have worked have described feelings of inadequacy when trying to support children using technology or trying to remedy hardware or software problems; others talked of their need to set aside time for trying things out and to make informed choices about purchases.

Some practitioners remain ambivalent about the value of ICT for their practice, despite its use being endorsed by policy. At the beginning of our series of research projects we found that practitioners' experience with ICT was largely restricted to computers and educational software. They were comfortable with providing computers and CD-ROMs for children to use in the playroom, but they were much less likely to use DVDs, digital and video cameras or create and edit material on the computer. Very few practitioners used the computer and internet to support their own practice by seeking out materials, downloading resources, using email or recording their observations of children and building profiles, and they were often dependent on other colleagues, family or friends for assisting when problems arose: 'At the moment, we're not confident. If there's any problem we're looking at each other – press this button, press that button. We're not confident and we know we're not confident' (Elspeth, nursery class practitioner).

However, by the end of Interplay there was a shift towards more assured and independent use of technologies available in preschool settings, although this was still largely restricted to computers. Three-quarters of the practitioners had learnt to use their technology in new ways, for instance, accessing the internet with the children or using additional software. There was evidence of more use being made of digital cameras in the playroom: in our survey of practitioners the number reporting that they were using digital cameras had doubled in two years and those using a video camera had trebled. It was still only a minority who reported that they were now downloading, editing and printing photographs and playing back video they had recorded but, as their confidence grew, some practitioners talked about how they were becoming more aware of the possibilities that ICT offered and more comfortable with allowing children to use the technology that had been previously thought of as too expensive or complex for children:

> Using the camera and downloading the pictures, before we'd have been 'Oh, just wait a minute and I'll do it for you and I'll let you see them once they're done', but now we're just letting them have a go.
>
> (Janet, day nursery practitioner)

Children's encounters with technologies in the playroom

The free play period, when children choose activities from those set out by practitioners, makes up most of each daily session in the playroom. The use of technological resources was firmly placed in this period rather than during the daily small group or whole group sessions initiated by the practitioner. During the free play periods we observed examples of children following the nursery rules about how to take turns, of a rapid turnover of children and of queues forming for popular activities, but we have also seen ICT remain untouched throughout a session when children favoured other activities such as construction, role play or playing outside.

Some children seldom or never choose to engage with technology. Practitioners sometimes ascribe this to ample exposure to technology at home, but others see it as a reflection of children's individual preferences: 'Some are just not interested in the computer – they prefer other activities' (Lillian, nursery class practitioner). Other children were considered to spend too long on computer activities by practitioners keen to achieve a balanced curriculum. For most of their time in preschool, children can choose what to do and when to do it, so we have observed very different patterns of engagement. Some children, like Sian, chose to play computer games when they arrived each day.

Sian: Using the computer alone

Sian went immediately to the computer when she arrived at playgroup. She used the mouse to enter a game on the pre-loaded Milly's Math House and began to work through a counting sequence. She completed four more counting rounds then closed that game and selected another game from the same CD. The new game required her to match big/medium/little shoes with characters of the appropriate size. Sian matched the characters and shoes correctly on each of the nine rounds offered. The game ended and Sian chose a game in which the appropriate

---

number of items was counted to match a cash register key. She worked through the numbers one to ten, and then moved to numbers 20 to 30. In this round she moved through the numbers in a less orderly way and took her hand off the mouse for the first time since her computer session began. She rubbed her eyes then clicked on 29 and the audio track counted out 29 items. Sian began to look around and left the computer. She placed a doll in a pushchair and began to walk around the playroom. During her 15-minute session Sian had looked intently at the screen and had not spoken to another adult or child.

(Field note description of Sian at Lowland Playgroup)

Other children engaged infrequently, only with particular resources, or in order to play specific kinds of games. For children like Colin and his friends, using the computer was something they did together, although not without some rivalry.

Colin and friends: Using the computer together

As soon as story time was over at 10.55 a.m., three boys rushed to the computer. Colin took control of the mouse, telling Ben not to touch while Paul sat quietly alongside. Ben tried without success to find something on the monitor that would allow him to turn up the inaudible sound, but Colin repeatedly restrained him. Graham arrived at the computer. Unable to force his chair into the row established by the other boys, he sat behind them. Colin began the game that was on the screen. Ben left the computer area when Colin again told him not to touch and Graham quickly took Ben's place in the front row. Colin moved briefly to a counting game then selected a game that involved listening to musical instruments – a game that was clearly unsatisfactory given there was no audible sound. Now Greg arrived at the computer and tried to place a chair alongside the others. They ignored him and he was forced to sit behind.

Colin continued to move quickly between games. When he returned to the hidden picture game all the boys joined in trying to guess what might be concealed. As Colin moved on to a 'catch the shape' game, Greg asked to have a turn. Colin refused and Greg left. An argument ensued between Graham and Colin about the length of Colin's turn. In the course of the debate Graham appealed to an adult, but Colin ignored her request to give others a turn. The boys argued about who had had a turn on the previous day and who had spent most time on the computer since they began nursery. At 11.12 a.m. Colin passed the mouse to Paul, saying that he would have another turn when Paul was finished. Paul played 'catch a shape' while Graham appealed again to a practitioner who replied that it would be Graham's turn next. At that, Colin and Paul left at 11.16 a.m. Graham took up the mouse and played two games briefly until 'tidy up time' was called.

(Field note description of Colin at Earltown Nursery Class)

When they were using a computer alone, we sometimes saw children intently engaged in a game, but others were easily distracted from the activity by things happening elsewhere or gave up when they could not achieve what they wanted to do. The ways in which practitioners respond to these varying patterns of engagement can be thought of as reactive or proactive. Proactive supervision involves planned interventions to introduce children to the use of resources or software. However, in our initial observation study we noted more reactive than proactive supervision: practitioners became involved in the activity only as a reaction to problems over turn taking, because their attention was prompted by noise or signs of mounting merriment or distress or when children asked for help. However, we did not see children asking for help very often. In these resource-rich environments they were more likely to abandon the technology and move to an alternative activity:

> Really the computer just sat there and it was an additional thing and it just sort of happened throughout the morning that everyone was inter-acting in all the other areas and it was left there. Basically, if there was a problem you'd go over and fix it then you'd leave. We actually felt a bit uneasy about the whole thing because it was the one area where if you came across and asked me how so and so was getting on at the computer I wouldn't have known.
>
> (Claire, children's centre practitioner)

Playing with technology: Five obstacles to successful engagement

ICT has been endorsed in the curriculum and included in the playroom by practitioners who see it both as an additional resource to support learning and as a part of contemporary life with which children need to engage. Children, too, are attracted to it. But we identified five main obstacles to children's lack of success in their encounters with ICT based on our observations in the playroom, which we outline here. In Chapter 5 we describe some further problems relating to the technology itself.

The first obstacle was that practitioners lacked the *time* necessary to support the use of technology. They needed opportunities to find and purchase the resources that were appropriate for their setting, time to help a child who was having difficulty simultaneously managing headphones, a book and rewinding a story tape or time to demonstrate the use of a paint technique in a drawing package. But playrooms are busy places and practitioners are usually responsible for supervising more than one activity. Making time for one-to-one interactions was not always achievable, and there were other demands for individual support competing for the practitioners' attention, such as reading a story or helping a child to manipulate scissors. In these circumstances, the prevalence of reactive supervision was an understandable response to the practicalities of the environment, even if it did mean that children's encounters with technologies did not always maximize their potential.

The second obstacle arose from the problems practitioners experienced when trying to *monitor* children using technology in the playroom. Computer screens are not readily visible across the playroom and children's interactions with technological resources are not easily observed in the process of casting an eye over the room that practitioners typically use to monitor play and levels of engagement (Stephen, Brown, Cope and Waterhouse 1998). For instance, the effective operation of an audio player cannot be observed and the communicative value of digital video may not be apparent when practitioners cannot hear conversations across the play area.

The third obstacle occurs when practitioners lack *confidence* in their own competency with ICT, a rapid response to assist children in a busy environment can seem a daunting task. In these circumstances, areas such as baking or block play, where practitioners feel that their supporting role is more intuitive, are likely to be given priority.

The fourth obstacle was the resource-rich nature of preschool playrooms. Cuban (2001) describes ICT activities as a 'benign addition' to the playroom. In other words, ICT has been brought into educational environments as a useful *supplement* to existing resources. Its use does not transform practice, however, and practitioners tend to perpetuate existing ways of working while accommodating the new technologies. Our evidence suggests that while technological resources are a welcome feature of preschool playrooms, there are always many other activities which children can turn to if their encounter with technology is unsuccessful. And leaving an unproductive encounter with technology may not be noticed if, as often happens, the child moves on readily, with no apparent distress, to engage with another learning opportunity.

The fifth obstacle related to the way in which practitioners typically understood their *role* in supporting learning with ICT. We observed practitioners offering sensitive and responsive scaffolding for children's learning, but the emphasis on child-led practice and the practitioner's role as a facilitator for children's exploration meant that staff were reluctant to be involved in what they could interpret as direct instruction or overly 'teacherly' behaviour:

Some of them need help to get themselves logged in . . . some of them needed help logging out, some of them needed you there – they didn't really need you but they wanted the support of you there. They sometimes need the support to turn it on, or get to the right bit. Or if the mouse's arrow is away they need a bit of technical support. And I would say they also need an adult beside them to extend them, ask some questions, helping them along. They also need an adult just to sort out any other wee niggles like who's sitting next to them.

(Dorothy, children's centre practitioner)

Sometimes children needed to be shown how to use something or be told what it could do if they were to have encounters with technologies that would benefit their learning. But there were there many ways in which staff could guide children's interactions without being overly directive.

Chapter 5

Support for learning with technology in preschool

Although we have been emphasizing the need to embrace a broad definition of technology so far, we focus on computers in the first part of this chapter because it was our observations of the problems that children encountered with them that led us to explore ways of providing support. It was only in the course of doing this that it became clear that the computers themselves were the origin of many of the problems, and that by thinking about technology in different ways it is possible to eliminate some of these difficulties. Having outlined these problems, we go on to describe an approach in which we combined meeting the aims of our research with providing opportunities for professional development.

Parents and practitioners often lack confidence in extending children's learning with technology. Some feel that their role is almost superfluous because technology's interactive nature means that children have their own, electronic tutor and so adult guidance is not necessary. However, our research suggests that these feelings can be misconceived: adults, and other more able partners, have a critical role in developing children's learning with computers and other technologies because children of this age are not usually able to derive maximum benefit without additional assistance. This support does not necessarily mean showing a child how to use a particular device. It can also mean providing support in ways that adults often do unthinkingly: showing interest, asking questions, making suggestions, laughing at the jokes or funny noises or just being there. Practitioners can also provide support in the form of suitable resources and setting up appropriate activities. The term we use to describe these various ways of providing support for learning with technology is 'guided interaction' (Plowman and Stephen 2007; Stephen and Plowman 2008).

As researchers, we shared with practitioners an interest in how children's encounters with technology could enhance learning, so we worked together in a process of guided enquiry. During this process, which took place over a year, we developed our concept of guided interaction based on actual events in playrooms and introduced the term to practitioners, jointly exploring the ways in which pedagogy could evolve, rather than allowing technology to determine practice.

Some problems with computers

As described in Chapter 4, our observations in the nursery led us to the conclusion that desktop computers are not necessarily the most appropriate technology for young children as they are designed for adults and for individual (rather than collaborative) use. They are used in a fixed location, they force children into uncomfortable postures because they are often on unsuitable furniture and the software or websites frequently rely on a child's ability to read in order to follow instructions or enlist help. Children sometimes struggled with using a mouse; although there are alternative means of input (e.g. touch screens), it was unusual for us to see these in use. Adults and children frequently referred to 'playing with the computer', but we found that boredom, frustration and disengagement were common responses to this activity, whereas fun, pleasure, spontaneity and enjoyment, the features associated with play, were rarely observable. Figure 5.1 shows a sequence of images of Josie 'playing' with the computer. The comic strip was based on video recorded during the research process with stills selected for key points of the action. In this example there is no dialogue because the girl has been left on her own. (In the other comic strips the actual dialogue is represented in the speech bubbles, using different shapes for the practitioner and the children.)

Josie has a game loaded but she has reached an impasse and after staring at the screen for a while she looks around for help. As that is not successful, she tries to solve the problem for herself and starts to click on the mouse again. This still does not work and so she abandons the approach, starts to scratch herself, then stares at the screen again. In the last two images we can see that she puts her head in her hands and then appears to give up, still staring at the screen and probably feeling bored and frustrated. It is noticeable that the computer is in the wrong position. Owing to a lack of space, it has been placed on top of the processing unit so that the screen is too high and she has to look up at it in an awkward position.

Figure 5.2 shows another example of some of the problems we identified with use of computers. On this occasion, a practitioner has set up the activity and has checked that Lauren remembers how to play the game before leaving her, but it becomes evident fairly soon that the girl does not remember what to do. As in the previous example, the computer is unresponsive when Lauren clicks the mouse. The video shows that she does this repeatedly (44 times). Because she does not get the result she wants or expects, she seems to assume that she is not using the mouse correctly. She tries hitting it on the table and that does not work, and she then tries putting the mouse flat against the screen. This action makes sense inasmuch as she knows that it is the mouse that controls what happens on the screen, but interaction with computers is rarely intuitive; it only seems that way once we have become accustomed to using them. For somebody who has not had much exposure to seeing people use computers, placing the mouse against the screen must seem a viable

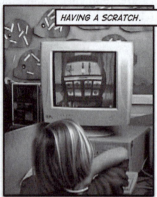

Figure 5.1 Playing with the computer?

Figure 5.2 Problems with the mouse.

option because there is no obvious mapping between the movement of the hand on a mouse and the movement of the cursor on the screen. This approach does not work either and she gives up, putting the mouse into her mouth. During this period the practitioner is busy elsewhere and does not have Lauren within her peripheral vision, so she is unaware of the problems being encountered.

There were some occasions when play was an appropriate term to describe interactions with the computer: when playing together, and sometimes when alone, children exclaimed at their success, called for others to look or laughed at an animation or a goal achieved. Some children deliberately completed a task incorrectly if they enjoyed the response of the screen-based characters telling them to try again, but these more playful interactions were relatively unusual. More often, we saw hurdles of the kinds illustrated in the comic strips. These incidents usually resulted from a combination of factors, some of which were directly related to the technology and some of which were related to the learning environment. In the examples provided here, the mouse appears to be an unsuitable peripheral to use as a pointing device for children with this level of computer experience and there is no way to advance the game without it. The frequent clicking has led to the screen freezing so, however much Josie and Lauren click, it is not going to resolve the situation. We do not investigate the problems with the design of the hardware and software here – although there is no doubt that more could be done to improve products for children in this age range – but we focus on the obstacles to successful engagement that are susceptible to being tackled by practitioners. In these two examples, the problems are exacerbated by the lack of human help, lack of appropriate resources and lack of experience. Together, these conspire to defeat the children's endeavours.

Our analysis centres on the ways in which adults can provide guided interaction. We might prefer children to be involved in guiding interaction for each other, as they would benefit from collaborative learning and it might result in fewer demands on practitioners' time, but our video analysis and observation demonstrated very few instances of children supporting each other in their uses of technology, as discussed further in Chapter 7. The principles of playroom practice are based on child-led activities in which children learn through play and exploration, supported by practitioners who monitor and facilitate rather than teach or direct. While there are many strengths in this approach, the examples of Josie and Lauren playing with the computer showed that existing playroom practice was incompatible with getting the most out of encounters with technology. Practitioners are experts at providing responses which are intuitive and finely attuned to children's specific circumstances and abilities, but this can be more difficult when ICT is involved. When children played on their own with computers we noticed episodes of use could be as little as 30 seconds, and typically it was no more than a few minutes before a child encountered a problem which would lead to them abandoning the activity. We also noted the obverse, in which children found a game with which they were familiar and would repeat it frequently if they had the opportunity. In either case, as described in Chapter 4, computers had to be situated away from mainstream activities like sand and water, and were often in a quiet corner so the lack of visibility made it difficult for staff to assess the situation. Combined with practitioners' underestimation of their role, this meant that the most common form of support was what we called 'reactive supervision', an intervention that was prompted as a reaction to an explicit call for help or a situation that demanded attention rather than one that was initiated by the adult. Children did not routinely ask for help and so the examples provided in the comic strips, in which children persist in their difficulties, were not unusual.

Of course, some children were able to enjoy their time with computers and knew what they were doing. However, over the period of our observations in playrooms we were struck by how frequently children encountered difficulties. In addition to the five obstacles outlined in Chapter 4, the reasons for this can be summarized as follows:

- The technology may be unsuitable.
- Children are reluctant to seek help from adults when they need it.
- Children tend to compete for time at the computer rather than collaborate with each other.
- Both children and practitioners lack confidence and experience.

Even though adult help was, in principle, always available, our observations suggested that children's interactions were neither productive nor particularly enjoyable and that they wandered off to find a more rewarding activity if the computer did not maintain their attention. It became apparent that the solution was not solely technological: young children needed both interaction with a skilful and sensitive helper to guide their interactions with the computer and access to technologies that were suitable for their interests and capabilities.

Guided enquiry

Having observed these problems, the research project Interplay was designed to explore ways in which practitioners could respond to change and create opportunities for learning with ICT while maintaining a balance between child-initiated and adult-led activities. The research led to us challenging the widespread belief that free play is a sufficient condition for learning and emphasizing the importance of the practitioner's role in guiding interaction.

As part of this project we devised an approach that gave the practitioners an active role in the research, rather than seeing them simply as informants, and we described this as 'guided enquiry'. We used this term because, as researchers, we were guiding the practitioners to identify problems and how they could be addressed, but we wanted to avoid the deficit approach to educational change which imposes solutions; our findings had to be rooted in authentic settings if they were to have any credibility with practitioners or any claim of relating to the dynamics and constraints of playroom experiences. Our starting point was to preserve the distinctive qualities of preschool provision, such as the emphasis on learning through play and child-led activities, and to acknowledge the expertise of the professionals who worked in the nurseries.

This process of guided enquiry is outlined in Appendix 2. It enabled practitioners to see how their current practice could constitute guided inter-action and raised awareness of how small changes could lead to enhanced learning. Although it was new to them, 'guided interaction' was a term which made sense to practitioners, so they were able to use the concept to reflect on practice and explore how they could enhance children's learning with tech-nology. Our intention was not to be prescriptive, but to use the concept as a way of supporting practitioners to use their own experience to identify opportunities for learning that may otherwise have been missed. In this way, it is consistent with an approach which sees relationships and interactions as lying at the heart of all learning experiences.

Our approach was to start from existing practice, observing the ways in which practitioners supported learning in other contexts and identifying the strategies that could be adapted for activities that involve technology. For instance, an observation of an adult showing two children how to make cookies (see Figure 5.3) revealed that in a situation which does not involve technology and in which they feel comfortable, practitioners will guide children's inter-actions, confident in their own competence and without worrying that they are being too directive. In this example the practitioner uses a range of objects, including cookie cutters, baking trays, a rolling pin, ingredients and an oven. She uses explicitly instructional language (i.e. 'Squeeze it together', 'Squash it into a big ball' and 'When you've cut out your biscuits'), introduces vocabu-lary (e.g. 'crumbles', 'baking tray'), engages children in learning conversations (e.g. 'Can you guess what we've got to do now?') and models behaviour by reading the recipe book and kneading the dough. The commentary in the caption boxes indicates some of the ways in which the children's inter-actions are being guided and is the outcome of discussions with practitioners during the process of guided enquiry, combined with descriptors from the taxonomy of guided interaction described later in this chapter. This cookie-making activity was recorded early in the study and was selected to show that engaging children in learning conversations and modelling behaviour are actions that can be appropriate and often come naturally to practitioners. Examples such as this are useful for making explicit responses and actions that had not been visible to us at the moment of recording as they enable us to isolate activity. The comic strips could then be used as the basis for discussing the forms of support that could be adapted for situations in which technology was a focal activity.

Figure 5.3 Making cookies.

As Alexander (2006: 11) puts it, 'It is true that children learn regardless of the intention of their parents, carers or teachers . . . But learning to a specific cultural purpose requires intervention and support by others'. It is the nature of this 'intervention and support by others' which we have conceptualized as guided interaction and describe in more detail here. The concept of guided interaction was mobilized to focus thinking about how children's encounters with the computer and other forms of technology can be enhanced and actively supported.

Supporting learning with technology: Sociocultural approaches

The sociocultural approach which underpins our understanding of how children can learn with and through technology was outlined in Chapter 3 and is developed here as we consider how factors such as the cultural practices of the environment, the material resources available and the role of adults shape the ways in which young children's encounters with technology are supported. As we use guided interaction as a way of conceptualizing support for learning with technology, we start by discussing how this fits within a sociocultural framework.

Chapter 4 outlined some of the ways in which responsive adults support learning: suggesting new ways to think about problems, deconstructing tasks into smaller units and providing physical support. It is not only interactions with technology that benefit from this support, as is made evident when we see children getting help with tying a doll's shoelaces or mixing paints. However, ICT presents a particular combination of operational and content challenges, so it differs from most resources found in the playroom. This means, particularly for computers, having to learn how to operate the technology before being able to benefit from its content. This was demonstrated in the examples of Josie and Lauren trying to play a game on the computer: they did not get as far as interacting with the game because they could not get the computer to function. This does not happen with sand or water play because the interaction is more immediate and the materials themselves suggest how they could be used. Even if we argue that children need to learn how to operate a book or a pencil, they can still get pleasure from the experience of looking at the pictures and pretending to read or from their emergent writing before they have fully conquered the operational requirements; the design of the book or the pencil does not impede interaction, but facilitates it.

Our observations suggested that technology can alter learning relationships more than traditional resources, such as a play house, building blocks, drawing materials or jigsaw puzzles. It was therefore useful to think differently about interaction with technology because it can require a greater degree of guidance than some other resources. Whether the person in a teaching role is a parent, a sibling or a practitioner at the nursery, introducing technology into the teacher–learner relationship inevitably alters the mediation of learning. The need to know how to operate some technologies before going on to benefit from the content has led to an overemphasis on the operational aspects, and we found that many nurseries did not get beyond thinking in terms of mouse control. While this is fundamental, as the examples of the girls trying to play a game on the computer demonstrate, developing children's competences with technologies extends beyond the operational aspects of how to use technology to include understanding its role in work and play.

There are many ways to conceptualize supported learning within the Vygotskyan tradition, which underpins this study and is outlined in Chapter 3, including scaffolding (Wood, Bruner and Ross 1976), assisted performance (Tharp and Gallimore 1989), dialogic enquiry (Wells 1999) and guided participation (Rogoff, Mistry, Göncü and Mosier 1993). These all use the concept of the Zone of Proximal Development (Vygotsky 1978), which proposes that children's development requires adult guidance or collaboration with more capable peers for challenge and support, to inform the ways in which they think about learning. The related metaphor of scaffolding describes the means by which children's competences can be extended by providing supporting structures which will eventually be taken away. These different ways of thinking about support for learning have emerged from the same tradition, so it is not surprising that they have in common the following features:

- the supporting role of adults or more competent partners;
- the verbal and nonverbal means by which adults guide children;
- the verbal and nonverbal means by which children seek guidance;
- the role of material resources and how they mediate learning;
- a focus on interaction as a dynamic, reciprocal process which is highly contingent on the activity, the participants and the situation.

These five features are also central to guided interaction. However, there are four key differences in the ways in which guided interaction extends these ways of conceptualizing support for learning in the particular contexts of technology and preschool environments that we describe.

- The concept of *task performance* underlies these approaches to supporting learning, but the concepts of both task and performance are inappropriate in the free-play context of preschool. Guided interaction focuses on the process of play and learning rather than the successful achievement of a task.
- The main mode of scaffolding and other forms of assisted learning is generally *spoken language*. Guided interaction is enacted multimodally, through different modes of interaction such as gesture and expression as well as talk.

- Scaffolding, assisted performance, dialogic enquiry and guided participation tend to focus on the immediate learning environment. Guided
  interaction shares this focus but also refers to practice beyond face-to-face
  encounters, in the *distal dimension*, to encompass elements in the wider
  setting such as planning, the provision of resources and concepts of role.
- The 'interaction' in 'guided interaction' refers to interaction with *technology*, as well as interaction with the environment and other people.
  Technology-mediated learning requires specific forms of support, but our
  observations revealed that explicit scaffolding, while common practice in
  other curriculum areas, was noticeable by its absence in relation to ICT.

What is guided interaction?

The concept of guided interaction as developed in Interplay provided a tool
for thinking about the different modes by which learning can be supported in
preschool settings and helped practitioners to articulate, reflect on and
legitimize changes in pedagogy. As it was elaborated in partnership with
practitioners, it seemed likely that the term 'guided interaction' might be
restricted to formal learning environments, but during our subsequent research
it became apparent that the concept could also be used to think about the
ways in which learning with technology is supported in the home, as
described in Chapters 6, 7 and 8.

In Tables 5.1 and 5.2 we provide a classification of guided interaction broken
down into the different types of support, the different modes in which that
support is enacted and the type of learning with which the support is

Table 5.1 Characteristics of guided interaction (proximal, direct interaction)

Proximal (Direct interaction)			
Form of guided interaction	Example	Mode	Learning
demonstrating	how to use a tool such as the paintbrush or eraser	physical action; oral	
	placing a hand over child's hand as they move the cursor or click on icon	touch	
	how to frame a picture in viewfinder	touch; oral	
	how to plug in electronic keyboard	physical action; oral	operational
	turning over pages of story as children listen on audio tape	physical action	
	waving hand in front of EyeToy	physical action	

Form of guided interaction	Example	Mode	Learning
enjoying	sharing pleasure in features such as animation	oral; laughter	learning dispositions
	moving to the music on a CD player	physical action	knowledge of the world, learning dispositions
explaining	what is on slides for the computer microscope	oral	knowledge of the world
instructing	reading dialogue box on screen	oral	
	tell child how to use digital camera	oral, gesture	operational
	tell child to push button on tape player	oral	
managing	intervening in turn-taking	oral; facial expression	learning dispositions
modelling	putting on headphones to check sound level	physical action; oral	operational
	using a play phone to order a taxi	physical action; oral	knowledge of the world
monitoring	moving child to appropriate level of difficulty	gesture; oral	learning dispositions; operational
prompting	suggesting a child tries something new	oral	learning dispositions
	helping with typing in names (typically to start a new game)	oral; typing	operational
providing feedback	giving encouragement for efforts	oral	
	smiling as child types name on keyboard	facial expression	learning dispositions
	says 'That's beautiful' when child shows picture on camera	oral	
supporting	stays close to child using video camera for safety and emotional support	physical presence	learning dispositions; operational

Source: Plowman and Stephen (2007: 19). Reproduced with permission of the publisher.

associated. We have also provided examples to illustrate what guided interaction looked like in practice, all of which have been taken from data collected during this study. Some of the data is from children's use of computers and some of the data is from other ICTs. More information about the ways in which we analysed the video data to arrive at the taxonomy of guided interaction presented in the tables is provided in Plowman and Stephen (2007, 2008).

Table 5.2 Characteristics of guided interaction (distal, indirect interaction)

Distal
(Indirect interaction)

Form of guided interaction	Example	Mode	Learning
arranging access to ICT	using sand timer to structure turn-taking	practice	learning dispositions
	recording patterns of use	policy	
ensuring access to help	making adult (or peer) help available	practice	learning dispositions
	checking on levels of engagement	practice	
modelling	using technology for a purpose, eg making video to show at parent's evening	practice	knowledge of the world
monitoring	planning child's return to activity	policy; practice	knowledge of the world, learning dispositions or operational
planning	ensuring balance across the curriculum	policy	knowledge of the world, learning dispositions
	ensuring range of activities for each child	policy	
	identifying learning needs	policy, practice	
providing resources	making broader range of ICT available	policy	knowledge of the world, learning dispositions, operational
	including disposable camera in story sacks for taking home	practice	knowledge of the world, learning dispositions
setting up activities	changing location and presentation of listening centre	practice	learning dispositions

Source: Plowman and Stephen (2007: 18). Reproduced with permission of the publisher.

Proximal and distal dimensions of guided interaction

Our analysis of preschool learning indicated two main dimensions of guided interaction. In the *proximal*, or face-to-face, dimension (see Table 5.1), guided interaction was most apparent in the interactions between adults and children that have a direct influence on learning and are usually visible. However, observations in the playroom and interviews with practitioners suggested that the planning of curriculum, the provision of resources and the role of the environment also played key roles. These activities guided interaction but were more distant in terms of time and space, so they were operating in the *distal*, or less direct, dimension (see Table 5.2). The practitioners orchestrated learning through these more remote pedagogical actions, guiding interaction at one remove from the closely coupled interactions described as proximal, but nevertheless taking effect at the site of the child's learning. Preschool practitioners tend to prioritize the planning and providing role of the adult over direct interactions between practitioner and child – a principled, if implicit, practice which is the legacy of a Piagetian approach to understanding learning (Stephen 2006). At its most simplistic, this constructs learning as a natural process of growth for children (hence the metaphor of the kindergarten), so the pedagogical approach derives from a concern with children's progress through developmental stages or sees child-initiated free play as the medium for learning. In such circumstances, a focus on direct adult–child interactions can be interpreted as being too teacherly and is considered as inappropriate for preschool settings. This attention to the broader context of learning differentiates guided interaction from scaffolding, which tends to have a close focus on the activity itself.

The proximal dimension of guided interaction can be resource intensive because it involves establishing joint attention on a one-to-one or small group basis. Table 5.1 shows a prevalence of physical interactions, so they have been subdivided into categories such as touch and movement. The physical modality is mainly related to operational outcomes as practitioners typically show a child how to do something by actually doing it rather than using a verbal explanation. However, it is also related to dispositions for learning through physical manifestations of pleasure in learning or the ways in which the simple act of being there provides a source of reassurance for a child trying something out for the first time. Support for the operational aspects of using technology cannot easily be provided at a distance: it requires close attention to identify and meet needs that are not made explicit by the children and which cannot be noticed from afar.

Modes of guided interaction

The mode describes the means by which guided interaction is enacted, a form of communication between the practitioner and learner that mediates their interaction. In the proximal dimension the interactions associated with guided interaction were multimodal in nature, encompassing language, gesture, touch, gaze and physical action. These interactions were highly contingent on the activity, where the learning episode took place, the learner's level of competence and the individual practitioner. The multimodal interactions referred to here focus on communication between the adult and learner and do not address the multimodality of the technological interface (e.g. communication via a screen, mouse or keyboard).

This shift in focus, from the proximal to the distal, was originally prompted by our realization that dialogue did not have the dominant role in technology-mediated learning for young children that a sociocultural approach led us to expect. Video analysis and observation demonstrated that language was not important as a mode of communication as there were few examples of extended adult–child thinking and talking. Talk is a key medium for interaction in school classrooms and guided participation, scaffolding and dialogic enquiry tend to focus on spoken language as a means of channelling support. Alexander (2006: 5) summarizes this reliance on talk in formal education settings in his statement that 'it is through language, especially spoken language, that teachers teach and children learn'. He notes the preponderance of overdirective use of classroom talk in schools, but its absence was striking in our observations of learning with technology in preschool. Responsiveness to children's emotional states is central to the practitioners' role in these settings, so touch, gesture and eye contact are also important forms of communication.

In the distal dimension support is enacted through policy and professional practices. Policy and practice are overlapping categories as actions taken in order to comply with policy directives and curriculum guidelines include planning and recording children's learning, such as setting up activities to provide desired experiences and curricular outcomes. Distal guided interaction is not as easily observable as proximal interactions because, by definition, it takes place at a distance, away from the immediate learning environment. Our information on this therefore came from interviews with the practitioners or notes they made rather than from observation.

Learning and guided interaction

Our analysis of practitioners' accounts of children's learning suggested that technology was used to promote three main areas of learning: extending knowledge of the world, acquiring operational skills and developing dispositions to learn. These categories were not intended to be exhaustive and they do not include, for instance, learning through physical activity. Although we saw some examples of learning through physical activity, such as children using a dance mat or movement games performed in front of a Sony EyeToy (a camera attached to a PlayStation), these were exceptional. The introduction of the Nintendo Wii has led to interest in the potential for technology to encourage physical activity, but we have only seen this in homes so far. Guided interaction could support all three areas of learning described here, although operational learning was more readily supported in the proximal dimension.

• *Extending knowledge and understanding of the world* included what is referred to as 'subject knowledge' in schools. It encompassed learning in areas such as mathematics, language and knowledge about living things and places such as animals or volcanoes, typically gained through software, websites and talking books. At the time of Interplay, this category also included children's understanding of the role of ICT in leisure, work and play, but this was later expanded into an extra category following observation in homes.

- *Acquiring operational skills* referred to understanding the functions of items such as the mouse and on/off switches, as well as the ability to operate them, which often relies on motor skills. Operational competence also develops children's concepts of technological interactivity and demonstrates their understanding that taking an action can produce a response. Children usually needed adults to help them acquire specific operational skills, after which they could move on to become independent users.

- *Developing dispositions to learn* encompassed a range of affective, social and cognitive features of learning to learn which were given high priority in preschool settings. Our interviews suggested that the practitioners mainly conceptualized learning as supporting children's development as confident and self-directed learners and that this was a fundamental part of practice. ICT was perceived to have a role to play in this by increasing self-esteem and the confidence gained from success, as well as supporting independence and persistence in the face of initial difficulties.

Tables 5.1 and 5.2 each have a column headed 'Learning' as both the indirect activities and the face-to-face interactions result in learning, even if this is not explicitly articulated or immediate. These broad categories of learning were based on accounts by practitioners in preschool settings, both in interviews and in the notes on children's learning that they kept routinely. Once we conducted more research in domestic settings we became aware of a further important aspect of learning: *technology as cultural practices*. This was encountered infrequently in the playroom, although Figure 5.4 illustrates how this can work in a preschool setting.

Three examples of guided interaction in practice

The following extract from field notes illustrates some of the features of guided interaction. Over a period of time, we were able to analyse a whole series of events such as this in different locations, with different children and practitioners and with different technologies so that we could build up the detailed description of guided interaction shown in the tables.

Supporting play at the computer

Margaret sat beside Steven at the computer. He was interested in the Pingu programme but selected 'quit' by mistake. She helped him to get back to Snowball Alley and spoke encouragingly to him as he used the mouse to drag objects into position. Margaret asked Steven to count the number of snowmen and to repeat the numbers. He appeared to be totally absorbed most of the time but occasionally pointed to the screen or turned towards Margaret, looking very pleased. Margaret decided that John, who was hovering nearby, should join Steven. She changed the game to one suitable for two players and showed them how to click and drag. She sat on a small chair alongside the boys in a position where she could see the screen and the children. Once she could see that they had settled into the game she moved away, first telling them where she was going, and then scribbled down a log of the incident and which game they were playing on a sticky note.

(Field notes, nursery class)

As in the examples of Josie and Lauren, the context is a child playing a game on a computer. Again, the child has encountered difficulties, this time because he has accidentally selected 'quit', a design feature clearly not suitable for children who cannot yet read. On this occasion, the practitioner has spotted he has a problem and has sat down alongside him to help with both getting back to the game and the counting. Here, then, we have an example of *operational* support as well as *knowledge and understanding* as she supports the number work. But Margaret's assistance extends beyond this; by providing encouragement, as well as sharing Steven's pleasure in the game, she is providing support for *learning dispositions*. Changing the game to make it suitable for a pair of learners and showing them how to click and drag provides support for both operational learning and learning dispositions, but she also stays a few moments to watch their progress. In the space of a few minutes, the practitioner has seamlessly provided support for different forms of learning as well as supporting the boys simply through her presence, so Steven has enjoyed a considerably more productive encounter than Josie and Lauren. This support is provided proximally and includes a combination of spoken and nonverbal communication. The distal support is made by having the game available, although the field note does not tell us if Margaret was directly responsible for this and spent some time familiarizing herself with how to use it. By recording the incident on a sticky note for Steven and John's profiles, she is laying the foundations for future distal support so that she and other staff know that they have already spent some time with this game.

Although this is high quality support, it is also resource intensive as it starts with one practitioner for one child, changing to two children mid-session. Again, it was the operational aspects of using the computer rather than the numeracy content that prompted the problems. By extending learning to include technologies other than computers, it is possible to free up practitioner time for activities that may not need this level of proximal support or which can include more children. The second example of guided interaction, Figure 5.4, is not therefore based on use of a computer. Although this is also an example of proximal help on a one-to-one basis, the technology has been set up to encourage future independent use.

Nikki is using an audio-cassette recorder in what is known as the listening centre. This is one of the interventions that resulted from the guided enquiry approach. In this case, practitioners had chosen to explore ways in which children could enhance learning and pleasure from using an existing playroom technology which was often disregarded in favour of computers. The objects that have been provided to support the encounter include finger puppets for acting out the story of the three little pigs on the audio cassette, the book in which the story can be followed, dual headphones so that the practitioner can check what the child can hear and coloured stickers on the machine to indicate the buttons for stopping and starting the tape. Eileen, the practitioner, has noticed that Nikki is hesitating and has come over to check that all is well. She confirms that the right tape is in the machine, that the book is open at the right page and that Nikki has the headphones on. She uses the other headphones to make sure that the tape has started and repositions Nikki's headphones, although she takes them off again. Eileen affirms that the tape is playing and finds the right page again. Much of this support is *operational*, but this has been provided both proximally (by Eileen sitting down next to Nikki) and distally (by providing the resources of the stickers to show 'stop' and 'play' and by providing the other resources, such as the finger puppets and the books), to make this a more engaging encounter. Eileen models how to use the headphones and uses both verbal and nonverbal means of communication, supporting both *learning dispositions* and *knowledge and understanding*.

The next example includes a telephone as the focal technology, although it also includes a hairdryer. Shirley, the practitioner, is role playing being a customer at the hairdresser, with several children in service roles. She explains that she had booked a taxi but she is worried that it is not going to arrive in time, so she asks one of the assistants to phone and check that it is on its way. The boy phones the taxi and asks why it has not arrived. This is an example of children gaining fun and pleasure as they develop *knowledge and understanding* of the social and cultural uses of ICT. There are no operational problems, the resources are low cost and Shirley is able to engage with several children at the same time, suggesting the circumstances in which one might need to use a telephone, the operational requirement of knowing the telephone number of the person to be called and the cultural requirement of knowing what to say to the respondent.

These three examples – Margaret guiding two boys' interactions with the Pingu game on a computer, Eileen guiding Nikki's interactions at the listening centre and Shirley guiding several boys' interactions as they role played working at the hairdresser – give an indication of different types of technology

Figure 5.4 At the listening centre.

Figure 5.5 At the hairdresser.

and the different areas of learning that can be supported. Tables 5.1 and 5.2 are not designed to provide quantitative information on the frequencies of different types of interaction, but they can be used to make general observations about the pervasiveness of particular types of pedagogical action to be interpreted within this framework. Analysing guided interaction in this way is a means of both documenting and analysing learning, and it helped us to identify responses to two questions we posed at the outset of Interplay: How does guided interaction fit into a preschool culture of child-initiated learning through play? How can practitioners find a space for guided interaction among their many other responsibilities in the playroom? This framework enables practitioners to see that their existing practice can constitute guided interaction and there are no pedagogical actions here that they would find alien or uncomfortable. Rather, the process of guided enquiry raised awareness of existing practices and enabled practitioners to identify circumstances in which they could intervene and maximize opportunities for learning. It also enabled practitioners to identify times when a child's self-directed exploration is more appropriate. In these circumstances, the absence of action may in itself be the source of guidance.

Chapter 6

The home as a learning environment

Evidence from interviews conducted with practitioners at the beginning of the Interplay project suggested that practitioners had no firm information, other than that gleaned from conversations with the children or their parents, about how children engaged with technology at home. However, their participation in Interplay led some staff to begin to find out more about the resources that children used at home and what they were able to do with them. At some settings they added questions about using technology at home to the 'all about me' booklets or to the interviews with parents which occurred when children were about to begin nursery. Our interviews with practitioners revealed that they thought of what they offered in their setting as complementing and extending children's home experiences rather than recognizing that some children had more frequent access to more sophisticated resources at home. Some staff questioned whether the games children played at home supported learning or offered positive experiences; some also expressed anxieties that children might be spending too long playing computer games or watching videos at home, and this might affect what they wanted to do in nursery.

Children's experiences at home are, by nature, beyond the visibility of most practitioners and there are many misconceptions about these experiences with technology, as Chapter 2 demonstrates. It became clear that there was a need for information about the range of technologies available to children in the home, the kinds of activities they undertake and the learning this might facilitate, so we engaged in research that would enable us to find out more. Chapters 4 and 5 considered the learning environment of the preschool and then the types of learning with technology and how they were supported there; similarly, Chapters 6 and 7 describe the learning environment of the home, and then what children are learning from the opportunities they have to use different kinds of technology there.

Learning in the home

We start by considering what we know generally about learning in the home before moving on to consider the home as an environment for learning about and with technology. Although early years policy and practice now recognize that children's earliest learning experiences occur at home, we know surprisingly little about the home as a place of learning. For much of the twentieth century, researchers showed scant interest in what children might be learning before they started school. Partly, this was because academics and practitioners alike thought children were not ready to acquire basic literacy until they were five or six years old (Gillen and Hall 2003), and therefore believed that their earlier experiences at home would have little or nothing to contribute to understanding how children learn. However, following the Plowden Report (Central Advisory Council for Education 1967), which drew attention to the links between socioeconomic disadvantage and educational disadvantage, questions about differences in the home experiences of children from families with different socioeconomic status began to be asked.

In the last decades of the century, a number of landmark studies, both in the UK and in the USA, where similar concerns had been raised, set out to explore the impact of cultural differences on children's early learning at home and their preparations for school. For example, an influential study of the nature of conversations in the home between parents and preschool children (or, more specifically, between mothers and daughters) found that, contrary to the beliefs of contemporary educational experts, children in working-class families did not suffer from 'linguistic deprivation' (Tizard and Hughes 1984). This could not, therefore, be the cause of working-class children's poorer performance when they started school. Even more surprising at the time was the huge potential for learning Tizard and Hughes uncovered in the home lives of all the children participating in their study. Discussions preceding the study with early years practitioners showed that around half of them thought that parents made no contribution at all to their children's education in the time before they started nursery (Tizard, Mortimore and Burchell 1981). In the course of the study, it emerged that few staff thought it was worth finding out what the children were interested in beyond the nursery because they did not think that they had outside interests, or that if they did, these would have educational value.

In the conclusion to their book, Tizard and Hughes (1984: 249–254) argue that the home should be regarded as a powerful learning environment, listing the following kinds of learning:

- learning in relation to a wide range of general knowledge topics (including early literacy and numeracy), through play, games, stories and formal lessons;
- learning about family and community culture through discussion with others and by example;
- learning how to be a member of a family or community through conversations about the past of the family or community and the child's possible future life;

and these facilitators of learning:

- sustained parental attention to one, or a small number, of children, allowing for prolonged conversations and the development of advanced skills;
- meaningful contextualization of learning, within the wider world of family practices;
- close, intense relationships between parent and child.

For Tizard and Hughes, this last point is the key to the power of the home as a learning environment:

> It was a matter of great personal concern to most mothers in our study that their child should acquire the skills, knowledge and values that they believed to be important. It is this parental concern that converts the potential advantages of the home into actual advantages.
>
> (Tizard and Hughes op. cit.: 252)

The work of American cultural psychologist Barbara Rogoff explores the cultural factors that influence young children's development around the world. She draws attention to the ways in which universal routines and concerns of caregivers looking after young children (i.e. food, sleep, hygiene and shelter) vary according to the environment in which families find themselves. To take a very simple example, it is obvious that houses built in cold climates differ in many significant ways from those built in hot climates because the elements from which shelter is required are different. But she argues that from these fundamental environmental differences, cultural differences develop:

> Infant and adult mortality issues, shortage or abundance of food and other resources, and settled or nomadic life seem to connect with cultural similarities and variation in infant care and attachment, family roles, stages and goals of development, children's responsibilities, gender roles, cooperation and competition, and intellectual priorities.
>
> (Rogoff 2003: 9)

Even within a relatively small geographical area, differences in the environment and in the concomitant cultural contexts can produce very substantial variation in children's early experiences. Heath's (1983) immensely detailed, longitudinal account of children growing up in two working-class communities and one middle-class community in a rural area of the south-eastern United States shows that differences in both the physical and the cultural environment of these communities produced very significant differences in terms of children's existing competences when starting school. These competences included children's oral language skills and their perceptions of the purposes of literacy. Also, the ways in which they related to peers and to adults varied considerably from one community to another, and were clearly linked to their communities' histories, values and aspirations for their children.

Although children in 'Roadville', a white working-class community and 'Trackton', a black working-class community, lived in the same area and their homes seem, superficially at least, very similar (on the basis of photographs included in Heath's book), a crucial difference was that Roadville houses typically had two bedrooms, while Trackton houses had only one bedroom. In Roadville, children had their own bedrooms, with space for their toys and other belongings. They were expected to play there, and to keep their things tidy. In Trackton, all the family's clothes were stored in boxes under beds or hung on nails on the wall because the need to accommodate adults and children in the same room meant there was no space for a wardrobe. This resulted in no room for toys and an expectation that children would spend most of their time outdoors.

Typical play activities in the two communities were very different. In Roadville, children were given toys seen as appropriate to their age, such as rattles, cloth books or soft toys. As they got older, boys and girls were given different kinds of toys: dolls and tea sets for girls; plastic soldiers, cars and trucks for boys. These toys and toys chosen for their overt educational value (e.g. to match colours, shapes and sizes) were expected to be the main stimuli for play, with the stated aim that children should learn both gender-appropriate behaviour and prepare for school. Parents' interactions with their children in play situations often drew attention to the articulation of what was being learnt:

> When playing with a teeter pole [a pole on which coloured rings have to be stacked in size order], adults ask questions of the Q-I type: 'Where does this go?' 'Can I put this one here?'. Of parts of toys or pictures in books, they ask children to recite their names, attributes, and to repeat certain associated sounds.
>
> (Heath op. cit.: 136).

In contrast, in Trackton, babies and small children were not bought toys of these kinds, although they might be given 'temporary toys' such as car keys, buttons or spoons. Children spent much of their time outdoors, in interaction with other children and with adults. The kinds of activities in which they engaged were also gender-specific, but in quite different ways from the gendered play of children in Roadville. Boys aged 12 months and older were expected to engage in verbal and nonverbal challenges with other male members of the community. For example, adults might pretend to steal a toddler's bottle, and encourage a spirited response:

> Teasing through feigned hostility, disrespect, and aggressive behavior marks public occasions for practice in both nonverbal and verbal interactions. In Trackton, the audience demands reciprocity in communicative situations.

Children are expected to learn to pay close attention to non-articulated signals about the consequences of their behavior and to calculate adjustments in their own behavior in terms of how they may act.

(Heath op.cit: 81–2)

Girls also learnt complex verbal routines, but in different contexts. These included 'fussing', where female members of the community engaged in critical but inventive commentaries of the behaviour of others, and hand-clapping or skipping games in which creative embellishment of traditional texts or improvisation was prized. Although adults affected no interest in these games, which were taught by older girls to younger girls, they included elements which could be seen as preparation for more formal learning at school, such as counting and vocabulary sets.

Heath's study shows that even in two communities only a few miles apart, young children's earliest learning experiences were very distinct, and that the differences had their roots in the environment itself and in related parental and community values. In the later stages of her research, when the children from Roadville and Trackton started school, Heath found that their early learning had a significant impact on their understanding of school activities. For example, for Trackton children, who were used to improvising and embellishing versions of events that happened in their community, the factual accounts required for some types of school work proved challenging. For Roadville children, where 'telling stories' was equated with telling lies in their community and could be severely punished, the concept of fiction was difficult to accept. The 'stories' they wrote tended to be unembellished accounts of their daily lives, often with a moral element. As a result, both groups of children had difficulty in adapting to certain aspects of school work, and performed less well than children from the middle-class community, whose early experiences had been more closely aligned to the interests of the school.

The question of how preschool and primary practitioners might build on the learning which young children experience at home is the focus of research by Luis Moll and colleagues. They have explored ways in which young children gain access to the kinds of knowledge and skills valued by the communities in which they are growing up, developing the concept of 'funds of knowledge' (Gonzalez, Moll and Amanti 2005; Moll, Amanti, Neff and Gonzalez 1992). These are the intellectual resources which reside within a community and are passed on to children through the community's own social networks – not just their parents, but grandparents, aunts, uncles, cousins and family friends and the work colleagues of all of these people. Moll argues that preschool and primary practitioners not only need to understand the kinds of intellectual resources which young children are able to access within their communities, but they also have to build the curriculum around these resources, or children will find the kinds of learning offered in the early years incomprehensible or irrelevant.

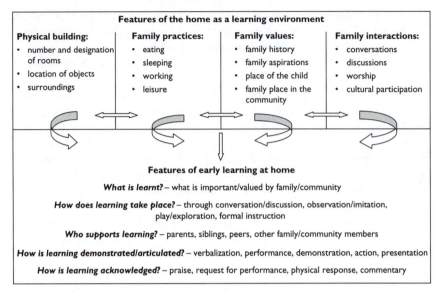

Figure 6.1 Influences of the home environment on early learning.

From studies such as these we can see that when we think of the home as a learning environment, there are a number of significant elements to be considered: the physical building, the routine practices of the home, the cultural histories, values and aspirations of families and the communities in which they live and the interactions within the family and with the wider community. All of these elements are linked to each other and combine to determine both *what* children learn – including what is seen as important or valuable – and *how* they learn. This is the relationship illustrated in Figure 6.1, and in the following sections we look at these different influences on the home as a learning environment.

The technological and sociocultural landscapes of the home

Digital technologies rarely featured in these seminal studies of homes as learning environments for young children, not least because most were conducted before computers, mobile phones and electronic toys were widely available in homes. Television and radio, of course, have a longer history of domestic presence, but they feature rarely in the studies we have reviewed. Although Roadville and Trackton families had televisions, Heath's passing references to radio and television broadcasts largely refer to adult listening and viewing; children from both communities watch *Sesame Street*, but there is no discussion of how or when they watch this, or what influence it might have on their learning. Tizard and Hughes note that early years practitioners believed that children spent most of their time watching television at home, but they found that fewer than half of the 30 children in their study watched television at all during the data collection period of two and a half hours. Those who did spent an average of 11 minutes watching TV during this time.

Items such as computers, games consoles, mobile phones, DVD players and technological toys of various kinds began to enter homes in the 1990s, and have become increasingly commonplace since then. Although there have been a number of studies investigating older children's home use of these technologies, particularly computers and games consoles, with a view to understanding their educational potential, there has as yet been little attention to the role they play in preschool children's home learning experiences. The two studies we have completed, Already at a Disadvantage? and Entering e-Society, and a third study, Toys and Technology, which is in progress at the time of writing, therefore have a contribution to make to the debates around the value of young children learning to use such devices.

These three studies set out to investigate the kinds of technologies available in homes, children's access to these technologies and the role these technologies play in children's home learning experiences. As we have noted in this book, the concept of toxic childhoods, in which technologies are seen to play a negative role in children's lives, is now extensively debated. In the 1980s, television was widely critiqued as the 'electronic babysitter' (Tizard and Hughes op. cit.). Now, computers and games consoles have taken the place of television as favourite *bêtes noires*. We wanted to see whether young children really spend extensive amounts of time playing computer games of various kinds to the exclusion of other traditional childhood activities, including outdoor play and social interaction with peers and family members, as alleged. If children did use digital technologies, we wanted to see what they might gain or lose from such engagement.

Physical features of the home as a technological environment

As Rogoff (op. cit.) and Heath (op. cit.) describe so convincingly, environmental differences lead to diverse cultural patterns. The physical features of the home as a technological environment therefore constitute important factors in our understanding of how children's learning with technology is supported.

Almost all preschool children are now growing up in homes in which a range of digital technologies are available. In a survey of children's use of digital technologies in the home that we conducted for Already at a Disadvantage?, all of the families responding to our survey had at least one television set and at least one video player. Almost all (96 per cent) had at least one mobile telephone and most (75 per cent) had a computer with internet access. In addition, these families possessed a wide range of digital toys, games and other technological items such as digital cameras, electronic musical instruments and MP3 players; some of these were purchased for their preschool children, while others belonged to older children or adults. Although we do not have comparable survey data from subsequent studies, our observational data demonstrate that the range of digital technologies in use in the home has grown considerably over the course of the decade – in particular, there are now more digital toys and games designed specifically with preschool children in mind – and, as prices for these kinds of items have fallen over this period, more families are able to buy them.

A significant change over this period has been the move from dial-up access to the internet to broadband. The *Oxford Internet Survey*, which has been charting British internet trends biannually since 2003, shows that among households with internet connections, the use of broadband has grown from 19 per cent in 2003 to 85 per cent in 2007 to 96 per cent in 2009 (Dutton, Helsper and Gerber 2009). For our families, this change has been significant. In 2003, families had to restrict access to the internet because dial-up was charged by the minute, and therefore the more time spent online, the higher the monthly bill. Broadband typically has fixed monthly costs, usually regardless of the amount of use, and therefore children's access is not restricted by cost. One consequence of this change has been the virtual disappearance of children's CD-ROMs which, at the beginning of the decade, were widely sold or given away free with toys, books and magazines. These were the main source of electronic games for young children at that time, but since broadband became established, children have been able to access games on children's websites.

The location of these items in the home makes a difference to the opportunities children have to use them. Families often have several television sets; the largest and newest set is typically in the family living room, while smaller, older sets with fewer additional features are usually found in kitchens and bedrooms. Some preschool children have television sets, usually with video or DVD players, in their bedrooms; in other families, parents have chosen not to make this kind of provision because they prefer their children not to watch television programmes or films alone or at night. Nevertheless, regardless of where they have access, by the age of three or four, most children are experienced watchers, able to identify favourite programmes and films and aware of the existence of a range of channels. They are learning to use the various television, video and DVD controls for different sets around the house, and parents usually encourage this growing autonomy which frees them from the need to change channels, insert DVDs, rewind or fast forward on demand.

The location of computers – and consequently the kind of access children have – is more varied. For families with one computer, its location needs to facilitate use by all family members, or at least by the main users. In some families, it is located in the living room, but in others, it may be in a study, a bedroom or a hallway. If one of the reasons for having a computer at home is to enable adult users to work or study, the living room is not ideal as these activities might be disturbed by television and other family leisure activities or by social visits. Location is sometimes deliberately chosen to limit children's access. Where parents work from home, using expensive equipment and specialist software, they may not wish to risk children damaging the equipment or altering or deleting work. In such cases, the place where the computer is kept may be out of bounds or only open to children on special, supervised occasions. In one family which lacked the space for separate accommodation for a computer, parents hid a laptop under the sofa in their living room and took it out for use only when their child was not present.

Items bought specifically for children, or which children are freely allowed to use, are found throughout the house, particularly in living rooms, play rooms and the children's own bedrooms. Many items (e.g. hand-held games consoles and electronic toys and games) are portable and easily moved to where the child wants to be. This means that children can play with them whenever they want, as is the case for other, non-technological toys. In general, we have not found that children prize technological toys over others: if asked to pick out favourite toys from those they have around them, they sometimes choose technological toys and sometimes choose others. Parents confirm that their children play with a very wide range of items and that both technological and non-technological toys may feature as the favourite for a while, but can be supplanted by others. While adults may contrast 'traditional' toys they recognize and played with themselves when young with newer, 'technological' toys, children appear to make no such distinctions.

Mobile phones, digital cameras and portable DVD players are similarly portable but may be stored out of sight, as parents usually see these as their own possessions or as items to be used under supervision. The use of mobile phones in particular tends to be limited, for reasons similar to the restriction on children's use of the internet when dial-up was the norm: calls are either charged by the minute or limited by the provider to a certain number per month, and parents need to avoid large bills. They are also concerned about children dialling random numbers, children accidentally calling emergency services and the health scares that occasionally surface in the media.

In addition to cost, technological complexity also affects children's use of different products. Almost all of the children had learnt to switch on the television themselves and could select channels, and they were learning to use video and DVD players, which entailed selecting and inserting discs or video cassettes and becoming more proficient with play, rewind and fast forward controls. Some could use on-screen menus to select programmes stored on hard disc, to check television schedules or to play interactive games. However, in comparison with mobile phones or computers, even the most complex television is relatively simple. Phones and computers have many more functions and ways of accessing these functions. Children need not only to understand

how to do this, but also to be able to undertake the activity to which they have
gained access, whether this is sending a text, playing a game or viewing stored
data such as photographs. For these reasons also, families tended not to provide
unsupervised access to phones and computers.

Some toys and games fall into this category, too. Large-screen and hand-held
games consoles represent a considerable challenge for small children. Not only
does it take time to learn to use the controls effectively, but many of the games
are designed for older children or adults, and speedy use of the controls and
fast thinking are required. It is not surprising then that young children find it
difficult and frustrating to attempt to play these games of skill, although they
are very attracted to them.

Family practices

A striking feature of children's use of technologies at home is the huge
variation in the kinds of activities children enjoy in this context. This finding,
which we have reported consistently across all the home-based studies we have
conducted, contrasts quite markedly with public perceptions of children's technological activities. There is a widespread view, as we have discussed elsewhere
in this book, that children (of all ages) spend most of their time playing video
games. It is also widely believed that they play these games in isolation, for
several hours at a time, to the detriment of more traditional play activities that
offer greater social and greater physical engagement. For preschool children at
least, this is not the case.

We have found, rather, that children's use of technologies, as with all their
home activities, are influenced by family practices in the home, such as sleeping,
playing and working. As we have seen, these are the purposes for which homes
are designed, but there are vast cultural differences in the ways in which people
engage in these activities, and practices differ among families and even within
communities. A comparison between two families who took part in Already at
a Disadvantage? reveals how different work practices in these homes influence
the children's technological experiences. Both families were classified by us
as disadvantaged: their household incomes were low and other factors, such as
disability or living in an isolated area, contributed to the limited resources at
their disposal. The ways in which the parents in the families made use (or not)
of technologies for work purposes influenced the kinds of technological
activities in which the children engaged, as illustrated by the vignettes below.

Shona: the internet as an educational tool

Shona was three years old on our first visit, and living in a village on the
outskirts of a large town in central Scotland with her parents and her
older sister, Moira, aged eight. Mr Wallace ran a small business from

home selling tropical fish, using the internet. Mrs Wallace was learning to use the internet, and email in particular, as part of an office studies course. She hoped this would allow her to find work more lucrative than the previous jobs she had held as a supermarket checkout assistant and an auxiliary nurse. They also used the internet to buy and sell second-hand goods.

Shona was thus growing up in a family in which the internet was seen as having valuable economic and educational potential. She and Moira spent considerable amounts of time online, visiting websites of interest to them – these included the Barbie website, websites relating to animals, and educational sites such as think.com. Moira was also an active user of a children's messaging system, an activity encouraged by their parents because she had, until recently, been a reluctant writer. Shona's mother saw these kinds of activity as educational, both because the children could acquire useful information from the websites they visited and because understanding how to use these kinds of technologies would be useful to them in later life.

(Field notes and interviews, the Wallace family)

For the Wallace family, the internet had potential for increasing household income as it was used to market the tropical fish business and had been used for buying and selling. Shona also made use of the web for her own purposes, enjoying both its educational and entertainment value. For the Newtons, who are described below, it was the hardware that provided scope to increase household income and the internet was of little value as they made use of local venues for buying and selling goods. Not having internet access, the parents and children found other ways of getting entertainment value from the computer.

Justin: exploring technology for entertainment

Justin was four years old when we first visited him, and living in a former mining village with his parents. He was the third of four children: he had an older brother aged 11, an older sister aged five and a younger sister aged two.

Justin's parents had had a computer with internet access in the past, but at the time of our first visit, had swapped the computer for a motorbike, as they had not found the internet connection useful. Mr Newton's work as a van driver and Mrs Newton's part-time job as an assistant in a burger bar did not require internet skills. Although they sought to extend the family budget by buying and selling second-hand goods, they did so through car boot sales, swapping goods with friends and neighbours and visiting discount warehouses. As a result of this kind of activity, Justin's family occasionally acquired second-hand technological items, including computers, scanners and digital cameras, which had no instructions. They had to work out how to use them by physically reassembling them or by switching them on and experimenting with what they found. Once they had been restored to working order and their entertainment value exhausted, the Newtons would swap these items or sell them.

On our second visit, they had acquired a computer with software which allowed family photographs to be posted into humorous scenarios such as on the farm or at the circus. It also contained sound files which, when activated, turned out to contain jokes about laughing cows. The Newtons found these highly entertaining and played the jokes over and over again during the course of our visit. The children were encouraged to explore the contents of the computer and Mr Newton showed them how to accomplish a wide range of relevant tasks – switching things on, finding activities through the use of icons, playing computer card games and so on – depending on what they needed and what was of interest. Though he vehemently denied that these activities were in any way educational – according to Mr Newton, education was something that happened at school, while home was a place for enjoying yourself – it seemed likely that the children learnt much about the inner workings of computers and other items from these experiences and that they would be confident about trying new technologies as they encountered them.

(Field notes and interviews, the Newton family)

Family values

The presence of technologies in the home does not necessarily mean that children have unlimited access to them. Two factors restricting access, as we have seen earlier, can be cost and technological complexity. Parents' views on young children's use of technologies and on the suitability of particular activities are a third, very powerful factor determining the extent to which their children make use of the technologies in their homes.

Views differed, depending on the technology in question. None of the parents in our study felt that children should not watch television at all, and most felt that children enjoyed and benefited educationally from the kinds of programmes they typically watched. The specialist children's channels and other programmes or channels of general interest – nature programmes in particular – were regarded as eminently suitable for child viewing. A few parents sought to limit the amount of time their children watched television, and some mentioned concerns about violence or frightening material, principally in programmes designed for slightly older children. Such parents might place some restrictions on viewing time or content or insist that the children only watched television in a shared family space such as a living room.

Concerns around mobile phones were different. As we have seen, parents tend not to encourage children to use mobile phones on grounds of cost and complexity. Some also worried about potential health risks, having read or heard press items relating to potential brain damage, cancer or genetic damage ensuing from excessive mobile phone use. But these concerns were largely abstract because parents rarely allowed their preschool children to use mobiles. Their main influence was on decisions about the age at which their children might be allowed to have a phone of their own: most parents of preschool children envisaged that this would be far off into the future, possibly when their children start secondary school at the age of 11 or 12.

When asked about young children's play with technological toys and games, most parents were enthusiastic about technologies in the home, and comfortable with their use. In a survey which we conducted with parents towards the end of Entering e-Society, we found that almost all felt that their children's use of technological items was right for their age and that playing computer games was harmless fun. When asked whether children might be missing out on more important things, if they played with technological toys and games, the majority saw this as a question of balance – too much could be bad for children, but these activities have their place:

> It depends on the balance – as long as they're doing other things and that's not all they're doing. Alex loves football and goes to training twice a week and loves to play outside. If he has a chance to go out and play he will forget about the computer – it definitely takes precedence.
>
> (Interview with Claire Simmonds, Alex's mother)

Many parents encouraged their children to learn to use different technologies because they envisaged a future for them in which confidence and skill with technology would be increasingly important.

The Stewarts: Committed to a technological future

Catriona was four years old when we first met her. She had a six-year-old brother. Her father, Mr Stewart, was a marine pilot. Mrs Stewart was involved in home care for the elderly. Her parents were experienced users of a range of technologies. Mrs Stewart gained a qualification in computing immediately after leaving school, and had worked in the past as an IT trainer in the health service. Mr Stewart also used specialist technologies associated with his work and had more recently become competent in the use of the home computer, which they used for online shopping and banking. They had positive views of technology in the future, expecting that many more labour- and time-saving devices would become available and believing that children should take every opportunity to develop the technological skills which would enable them to take advantage of these features.

Catriona was fully competent with TV controls and with a mobile phone and played computer games with her older brother. Her favourite activities included playing with dolls, painting, watching TV and playing computer games. By the end of our visits to her family, she could also find favourite websites on the internet, enjoyed the Dance Mat, decreed LeapPads and VTech toys to be too babyish for her and could take pictures with the digital camera. Mrs Stewart was pleased that she was 'not frightened' of technology. Her favourite activities continued to be painting and drawing, which she did both with paints and crayons and on the computer.

(Field notes and interviews, the Stewart family)

However, other parents were unconvinced that an early start would bring particularly valuable benefits, and a small number of parents were concerned that early exposure might be harmful. These parents tended to place a high value on what might be termed a traditional childhood, focusing on the potential threat to imaginative play, arts and crafts and outdoor activities which technological activities might pose. Sometimes this was because the parents had had negative experiences themselves with technologies in the past.

The Baxters: concerned about the negative impact of technology

Grace was four years old when we first met her and had a six-year-old brother. Her father, Mr Baxter, was responsible for the production of a local newspaper, while Mrs Baxter was a childminder. Both the parents had had early experiences of learning to use computers. Mr Baxter studied computing at school, enabling him to convince future employers that he had the technological skills needed for a modern printing system, while Mrs Baxter had learnt basic programming and the use of accountancy software packages to help with her parents' business. However, they had negative views of these early technological experiences: both felt they had wasted considerable amounts of time in the past acquiring technological skills that were now, given the huge advances in this field, no longer relevant.

Mrs Baxter was concerned that electronic games make children aggressive. She also worried that having internet access at home would encourage her husband to take up online gambling or become otherwise addicted to the internet. She believed that any technological skills that the children acquired now would quickly become obsolete and that there was therefore no need to encourage them to learn to use those currently available.

As a result, Grace had very limited technological skills: in contrast to almost all the other preschool children involved in our studies, she could not use the TV controls and she owned virtually no technological items, other than toy versions of a laptop and a CD player. Her favourite activities were playing with dolls, dressing up, playing outdoors and swimming. Mrs Baxter did not encourage any technological activity and described Grace as uninterested in these things.

(Field notes and interviews, the Baxter family)

Family interactions

For all commentators on the home as a learning environment, the nature and quality of interactions involving young children are a key factor in their learning. For many, interactions between children and parents, or more specifically between children and their mother (who is typically the main caregiver in the home), are the most significant. Bronfenbrenner makes clear that the principal dyad (conversational pairing) to be studied in this context is the adult and the child, although others may become involved, and he argues that such dyads are the most powerful factor supporting the child's learning in the early years:

> Learning and development are facilitated by the participation of the developing person in progressively more complex patterns of reciprocal activity with someone with whom that person has developed a strong and enduring emotional attachment and when the balance of power gradually shifts in favour of the developing person.
>
> (Bronfenbrenner 1979: 60).

Tizard and Hughes (op. cit.) focused exclusively on mothers and children in their work. More recently, Gregory and colleagues have broadened the field somewhat to look at the role of siblings (Gregory 2001) and of other significant adults such as grandparents (Kenner, Ruby, Jessel, Gregory and Arju 2007) or other older children or adults who live in the home or are regular visitors (Long, Volk, Romero-Little and Gregory 2007). Heath's work (op. cit.) takes a very wide perspective, looking at the community as a whole, and including conversations between children and other, unrelated, adults in the community as well as conversations in the course of play among friends. In all of these studies, analyses of interactions are the most immediate indicators of what and how children are learning, and how interlocutors shape this learning by paying attention to (or ignoring) issues which children raise, pointing to significant phenomena in the environment, or indeed by overtly setting out to teach something which they feel a child should know.

What role do interactions play in supporting children's learning about technology? The interactional data collected when we were observing children using technologies give some hints of the ways in which parents and children talk when the child is engaging in a technological activity. The following dialogues highlight two children who happened to be playing the same game, *Tamba's Travels*, on interactive television. The transcripts show how the conversation can focus on the operations of the game itself or on its content.

Ellie: Learning to play *Tamba's Travels*

MUM: Press the little button. You press the . . .

RESEARCHER: Now what do you do?

MUM: You need to . . . Now wait . . .

ELLIE: Ah . . .

MUM: Which one are you going to go on?

ELLIE: Mummy can you get it on Tamba?

MUM: You want it on Tamba? Press the up arrow, the arrow that is going up. Up. That's it. And then the middle button. That's it. Good girl.

RESEARCHER: So which one are you going to?

ELLIE: Tamba.

RESEARCHER: That's a game?

ELLIE: Yeah.

MUM: We haven't done this one before, have we? This must be a new one. *Tamba's Travels*.

RESEARCHER: You've never played this before?

ELLIE: No.

MUM: Right, press the middle button again, then. Ah now, can you write your name on this one? This is a tricky one you've chosen.

ELLIE: I know.

MUM: Right, move your arrows round until the yellow . . . this is going to be tricky. Press the down arrow, that's right, and then along until you get to the first one of your name, right, and then I think press the middle button. That's right and then move along and move down then along until you get that . . . umm. There's the . . . can you see it?

ELLIE: What then?

MUM: Yeah that's it, good girl. Right, press the middle again.

RESEARCHER: Well done.

MUM: And then again.

ELLIE: On there?

MUM: Yep and now you need to try to get up to the R using the arrows.

ELLIE: Where's the R?

MUM: It's in the top row. Good girl. Now . . .

ELLIE: Mummy.

MUM: Then I think you need to go up.

ELLIE: Why?

MUM: Right up to the top. That's it and then along and that's it and press the middle one again. I think that'll work. That's it.

ELLIE: I want a girl one.

MUM: Right so that's. . . . What colour do you think that one is for the girl, then?

ELLIE: Red?

MUM: Red, that's it. Good girl. Press the red button skin colour.

ELLIE: Same colour as me.

MUM: So what colour's that one then? It's the red button isn't it?

ELLIE: Yeah the red one.

MUM: Press the red one. Hair colour . . .

ELLIE: Same colour as mine.

MUM: Mmmm so what's it going to be, red or blue?

ELLIE: Red?

MUM: The blue one is maybe closer to your hair colour. You need to press the colour, darling, on that one. That's it. Ooooh, hello Ellie. Let's go travelling.

(Video transcript of Ellie and Debbie Mackintosh)

In this dialogue, we see Ellie deciding to play a game she has not played before. Tamba is a character in a children's programme called *Tikkabilla*, shown on the BBC children's TV channel, CBeebies. Related games are designed to support appropriate learning for preschool children, including colours and numbers, craft activities, stories and knowledge about the world; the programme has a particular focus on children in other parts of the world. Because she has not played the game before, Ellie needs help with setting it up before she can start to play. This involves entering her name, by choosing letters on screen, and then designing an avatar (an on-screen representation of the child): the child can choose the gender of the avatar and skin and hair colours to provide an approximate representation. Only when these steps have been completed can the game begin. From the interaction, we can see that Ellie needs step-by-step support from an adult who understands the game's conventions and can help with elements which are quite challenging to the child, such as identifying the letters of her name and clicking on them in order.

At the time this conversation took place, Ellie was just four years old and her mother estimated that she had been playing CBeebies games on interactive television for about a year. By the time of our last visit to the family, some six months later, Ellie was playing these games independently, both on interactive television and on the CBeebies website, using a laptop which the family had recently bought. In her last interview, her mother commented that children did not need to be taught how to use technologies as they just 'pick it up': 'They probably see you using them and just pick it up automatically anyway. I've never shown my kids how to use the TV or DVD, they just watch and pick it up' (Interview with Debbie Mackintosh).

Thus we can see that parents can be quite unaware of the extent to which they have supported their children's acquisition of the skills needed to use these kinds of technologies over a sustained period of time as discussed in Chapter 8.

In another dialogue, Cameron is also playing *Tamba's Travels* on interactive television. Cameron has played the game before, but his mother deals with the technical elements for him. She holds the remote control and presses the buttons: in the dialogue, the constant reference to colours is due to the fact that choices are made by pressing coloured buttons on the remote control, with reference to colour coded options on screen. Other than this, his mother's conversation focuses on the game's content rather than the technical elements.

Cameron: Playing *Tamba's Travels*

MUM: He's called Cameron. He's got the same name as you. We're going travelling. Press the button to start the game. My suitcase is all packed. I've got room for just one more thing. What do you want to take in your suitcase? There's a bucket and spade, a teddy bear, sunglasses or a kite. Which one would you take?

CAMERON: A teddy bear.

MUM: Right, can you see what colour the teddy bear is?

CAMERON: I don't know.

MUM: Well, look underneath the teddy bear. Want to go up and have a look. See what colour button's underneath the teddy bear.

CAMERON: Oh, press green. Press green.

MUM: OK then. What a great idea. Now we can really have some fun. OK? Do you want to go to Africa or India?

CAMERON: India.

MUM: You want to go to India. Right.

CAMERON: Press red button?

MUM: Yes, that's India. OK and you are going to go on a plane. Your tummy goes funny. Press yellow. There's the Taj Mahal. There are some stripey tigers. I love India. So do you want to go . . .

CAMERON: To the tiger.

MUM: Choice there, try again. Camouflage. Right, so we're going to go and see some tigers. OK? What colour do you want some camouflage.

CAMERON: Blue.

MUM: So if you were in the jungle would we see you wearing blue? So that's a nice colour. OK, let's get going. Do the select. Right. An elephant, OK. Oh, it's a good story. But it's Justin from *Tikkabilla*, from Tamba. You like Justin, don't you? I think he is on holiday. I think he should come with us too. Right, what would you like to do? Play a flute to charm a snake or fly a kite?

CAMERON: Fly a kite.

MUM: Right. What colour?

CAMERON: Um, blue.

MUM: Is it, are you sure?

CAMERON: No, yellow.

MUM: OK . . . is very good. You've got a flying carpet, climb a ladder or do you want to ride on a bike?

CAMERON: Ride on a bike.

MUM: OK.

CAMERON: This is difficult.

MUM: That's a special bicycle because you see the seats at the back. That's called a rickshaw.

(Video transcript of Cameron and Jacqui Taylor)

In this extract, Cameron's mother constantly articulates for him the elements of choice in the game by encouraging him to notice that a trip to India will involve a flight in an aeroplane, naming the Taj Mahal and tigers as features of the Indian landscape and drawing attention to the meaning of unfamiliar vocabulary, such as 'rickshaw'. She may also be making the more subtle point that blue camouflage will not be particularly effective in a jungle setting, though she does not pursue this. It is not clear whether Cameron understands the concept of camouflage, and he may well see this as a simple colour preference question, an interpretation which could well be reinforced by his mother's comment that blue is a 'nice colour'.

We can see from these two dialogues that Ellie and Cameron's mothers support their children's technological play differently. Ellie's mother seems to see her role as teaching Ellie to use the technology, with the intention that she should become an independent user over time. In contrast, as was apparent from our interviews with Cameron's mother, she wants to avoid him becoming an independent user because she worries that if young children acquire these skills, they will cease to engage in imaginative or active outdoor play, both of which she prizes highly. For her, technologies offer valuable opportunities for acquiring some of the kinds of knowledge which preschool children need, but their use needs to be tightly controlled. She does not think that children need to have developed technological skills before they start school:

> I don't think learning to use new technologies is relevant to starting school. Right now the main things are self-esteem and socialization. Technology is in our lives and children see that, but it shouldn't be an emphasis right now. I would much rather see him having friends round and playing and running about. They will learn how to use technologies anyway.
>
> (Interview with Jacqui Taylor)

Despite these views, by the time of our last visit, some six months after this interaction, Cameron was becoming a competent, independent user of both interactive TV and CD-ROM-based games on his parents' laptop. As in Ellie's case, Cameron's mother found this surprising because, she comments, neither she nor her husband had provided any direct instruction. She suggests that he might have learnt to use these from the nursery, from friends or perhaps by watching his parents: 'You don't realize how much you are saying or what they are picking up from you' (Interview with Jacqui Taylor).

Interactions with siblings and peers are also influential. Carey, aged four, and her older sister, Marie, aged eight, had a close relationship, with Marie playing a strong maternal role. She, rather than their mother, taught Carey to use the various technologies around the house, including the PlayStation 2 games console which had been a Christmas present for Marie and was located in her bedroom. In addition to the main PlayStation control, she had an EyeToy. Marie and her parents felt that the EyeToy was more suitable for Carey than the PlayStation control, which was too complicated for small children.

In the following dialogue, Carey and Marie, play a game, using the EyeToy, called *Wishi Washi*, which (inexplicably to adults) involves washing windows. In *Wishi Washi*, they have to clean windows by waving their arms in the air. On screen they appear to have various cleaning implements (e.g. dusters, sponges and buckets) and dirty windows are progressively cleaned. They played this game in Marie's bedroom, bouncing on her bed.

Carey: Learning to play *Wishi Washi* with her sister

MARIE: Right, we'll play that again.
CAREY: A fiver.
MUM: You stand in the, stand in the shape.
CAREY: Where? Wisssshy.

RESEARCHER: That's it. Ooh.

MARIE: . . . washing.

CAREY: Wissssh, wisssh.

MUM: She must know she stands in the shapes, Marie.

MARIE: It keeps coming and that.

RESEARCHER: Yeah it does, doesn't it.

MARIE: I'll try.

CAREY: Wheew. I'm sitting here.

MARIE: Wait. Yessss.

RESEARCHER: Aaaah.

CAREY: Weeee, *Wishi Washi*. Quick, get it.

MARIE: Oh, . . . this bit cleaning.

CAREY: Again, again.

MARIE: Who wants a sponge? Who wants a sponge? Yessss.

RESEARCHER: Yeah. That's what you have to keep doing. I was wondering how . . .

CAREY: That one's not cleaning.

RESEARCHER: Right.

CAREY: Whee.

MARIE: I'll try.

CAREY: Try all right, all right. Wait, wait, oh, come on, come on.

MARIE: Oooh . . . is really hard.

CAREY: This, bucket, bucket.

RESEARCHER: Oh!

CAREY: Bad bucket, bad bucket!

RESEARCHER: Ah, that's the game over. Oh well.

CAREY: Game over.

(Video transcript of Marie, Carey and Marilyn Stevenson)

The spoken interaction between the children here consists of a running commentary on things as they evolve on screen. Carey's interjections are largely onomatopoeic exclamations indicating enjoyment (e.g. 'Whee' and 'Wisshh'), while Marie notes the stages of the game, in which, for example, different buckets appear, sometimes full of dirty water ('bad buckets') rather than clean water, and the need to acquire sponges which make cleaning easier. In this way she draws Carey's attention to the elements of the game she needs to be aware of in order to gain a high score. Carey, however, seems unconcerned about scoring, caught up in the physical enjoyment of the experience.

The adults in the room – the researcher and the children's mother – are not familiar with the game and are trying to understand, and encourage the children to articulate, what they need to do to play it effectively. Carey's mother has understood that Carey is failing to score points because she is not standing in the correct place; significantly, she asks Marie to explain this to Carey rather than telling Carey herself. In a subsequent interview she makes clear that Marie is the teacher, because she herself does not understand how the PlayStation works: 'Carey wouldn't ask me because I'd be really snookered' (Interview with Marilyn Stevenson).

Carey confirms this. When we show her a picture of the EyeToy and ask how a fictional child, Lucy, might learn to play with this, she says:

> That's an EyeToy, my sister has one! I recognize the camera! It would be quite easy for Lucy to learn to use it because my big sister has got one and you just press the little button and the EyeToy comes up and you choose 'EyeToy 1' or 'EyeToy 2'. You just wave and it loads up and then you wave again. Lucy could ask her big sister for help with it because I ask my big sister for help.
>
> (Conversation with Carey Stevenson)

Marie's interactions with Carey as they play the game are aimed neither at teaching Carey about how to use the technology, nor at identifying any educational content, as was the case with Ellie's and Cameron's mothers. Both children are concerned principally with enjoying the game on their own terms: Carey with the physicality of the experience and Marie with winning, which simply means prolonging the game. If they fail to clean the windows quickly enough, the game comes to an end.

From these extracts we can see that there are several different kinds of learning promoted by the technologies children encounter at home: learning to use technology, learning via the medium of technology, learning that learning itself is enjoyable but also challenging, and learning the role of different technologies in family and community contexts.

Chapter 7

Learning with technology in the home

In this chapter we consider in more detail what young children are learning as a result of their encounters with technology at home. As our starting point, we use the forms of learning with technology that we identified as part of our research in preschool settings and described in more detail in Chapter 5: acquiring operational skills, extending knowledge of the world and developing dispositions to learn. Here, we provide illustrations of these different forms of learning in the home and add another: learning about technologies as cultural practices.

Operational skills

Operational skills – the ability to switch technological items on and off, rewind, fast-forward, record and store and retrieve data – are the forms of learning most immediately obvious to adults considering what young children might learn from their experiences with technology. For example, early years practitioners often identify use of the mouse, and the related hand–eye coordination this requires, as a key learning gain.

It is undoubtedly true that children acquire these skills through their encounters with different technologies, and that, for young children, these can be physically and mentally demanding tasks, at least to begin with. Our visits to three- and four-year-olds in the course of our research have found children at various stages of competence, depending partly on their age and manual dexterity and partly on the extent to which they have been allowed to handle technical equipment themselves. Cameron acquired these skills at a later age than Ellie, for example, partly because his mother deliberately restricted his access to controls. The same was true for Grace, who was not encouraged to take an interest in technical items around the house but rather to ask her parents or older brother to do these tasks for her, to the extent that her brother was described as 'Grace's remote control' on one occasion.

In contrast, children such as Ellie or Carey, whose parents were keen for them to become independent users of domestic technologies, acquired these skills more quickly and, by the time they started school, could use a range of remote control devices and other items with confidence. They were unafraid to experiment when things did not work as expected.

Carey: What to do when the remote control does not work

Carey can use the television, with the remote control, but it hasn't been working for a few weeks. She explains what you do in this situation:

CAREY: Do you know what? My Dad can fix it by pushing every button.

Carey volunteers to give a demonstration of what she would do to turn on the TV using the remote control:

CAREY: Pretend I was coming in tired from nursery . . .

She jumps onto the couch and points the remote control at the television.

CAREY: . . . and I pressed the button and it didn't go on, then I know what button to press, I press every button.
RESEARCHER: And does it work when you press every button?
CAREY: Sometimes . . .

(Conversation with Carey Stevenson)

In addition to manual controls, children also have to learn to use on-screen controls, which include icons, menus and written instructions. These tend to be more complex than the manual controls, and again we have seen children at various stages of competence with these. By the age of five, many children are familiar with the concept of icons: parents frequently use these as a way of enabling children to access favourite websites which they bookmark for them on the family computer. Many can also navigate menus, particularly in relation to games with which they are familiar, although they may need help with new games. Written instructions present more of a challenge, particularly as very few children of this age can read. They may need their parents or others to read these or they may ignore the instructions and try to play the game without consulting them. Another common approach to this problem is to consult more experienced (possibly older) players of the game:

Freddie: What to do when a game is too difficult

About a month before our third visit to his family, three-year-old Freddie had been give a Nintendo DS. Playing with this was now his favourite activity. He played with it everyday, spending about two to three hours a day on it altogether, on and off in the course of the day. He often played with it in the evening when his older brothers (he has four, aged between 7 and 14) were watching TV, sitting on the couch with them and playing while they watch.

His mother said that he could play all the games he had for it, but was better at some than others. She said she had not shown him how to play, but Hamish, one of his brothers, comments that Freddie copies him. When asked if Freddie asks him for help, Hamish answers that he does. If Freddie gets stuck at a game he will give it to one of his brothers to do. When he gets frustrated and his brothers are not around to help him; he will put it down and go back to it later. His mother does not help him with the games: she does know how to play, but has no interest in them. She says that if she showed him how to do something once, she would be inundated with questions, so she just says no, and he does not ask her for help any more.

Just at this point in the discussion, Freddie got to a hard part of the game, passed it to Hamish, who got through the hard part for him and then passed it back to Freddie to continue playing. This whole exchange was completely wordless.

(Field notes and interviews, the Dawson family)

Extending knowledge of the world

Many parents, like Cameron's mother, see technological toys and games as ways of helping their children learn more about the world around them and, more specifically, of acquiring basic literacy and numeracy in preparation for starting school. The marketing of technological toys and websites designed for young children places considerable emphasis on the learning gains to be made. For example, the CBeebies website has an extensive section on how children learn, and uses icons to indicate the aspects of learning promoted by the games, such as 'Active Fun', 'Imagination' and 'Playful Learning'. Most of the children involved in our studies had at least one toy laptop or games console which made similar claims about the benefits they offered. These include LeapPads, interactive books with 'magic pens' which read the text aloud when touched on words, to support children's early attempts at reading; Leapsters, designed like hand-held games consoles, but whose games support the acquisition of phonics and knowledge of shapes, colours, numbers and basic mathematical concepts; and the VTech Smile Learning System, which similarly mimics a hand-held games console and, according to the VTech website, encourages children to play educational games which stimulate cognitive development, cooperative play, musical creativity and memory, among other things.

Although we saw children playing with these toys and games, it was difficult for us to determine the extent to which children were really making the learning gains claimed by designers and manufacturers. This is partly because our studies did not set out to test these claims systematically – and even if they had, it would be difficult to design studies which could prove cause and effect over time. Our impressions, when we saw children engaging in this kind of play, were that it was more difficult than the manufacturers implied to use these toys and games effectively as educational tools. Some technological toys designed for small children similarly require a degree of adult supervision, not so much because of the technological demands (though children may also need some time to get used to the controls) but because of the intellectual content. Many toy laptops and hand-held games designed for young children are marketed to parents on the basis that they are 'educational'. In practice, this often means that they focus on early numeracy and literacy skills, including basic arithmetic and spelling. However, most three- and four-year-old children are just beginning to encounter numbers and letters, so they are not ready for the kinds of tasks set by the games. We have seen games which asked children to add and subtract double-digit figures or to spell out words on the keyboard when they are still learning to count and to recognize letters. These experiences can quickly lead to frustration and the abandonment of a toy which fails to live up to its early promise, although children can make use of these toys in the intended fashion if more able others pay close attention to what the children are doing and provide help when the task becomes challenging. When children are left to their own devices with these toys, they may quickly tire of them.

Observation of a child who was a successful learner in a number of ways revealed several factors contributing to effective learning with technology. These included the opportunity to play games which appeal to and extend the child's existing interests and design which facilitates play but is not heavily reliant on written instructions or complex actions and yet includes intellectual challenges. In this case, four-year-old Alex was playing a game he had found on the BBC's *Question of Sport* website (BBC 2009). The *Denise Lewis Heptathlon* is a game in which cartoon athletes, including the Olympic gold medallist Denise Lewis, take part in a series of track and field events, accumulating points as the event progresses. The game was designed as entertainment for adults, but the cartoon athletes and the simplicity of the game appeal to young children. Alex was a sports fan – a keen swimmer, footballer and snooker player who also watched many events on television – so it is not surprising that this game, on a sports website, appealed to him.

During a visit from the researchers, Alex demonstrated how to play the game, which had the potential to support his learning in various ways, including early literacy, numeracy and knowledge of the world.

Alex: Extending knowledge of the world

Alex is sitting at computer with his right hand on the mouse, looking at a screen with choices displayed. He makes a choice and another screen is displayed. He continues to go from screen to screen. He finds the site for the *Denise Lewis Heptathlon*. He clicks to go from screen to screen and on buttons to select exactly what he wants to do. He presses keys on the keyboard to make the figure run.

ALEX: It's um it's the Olympics.

RESEARCHER: Right, now, is this going to be running?

ALEX: Yes it's got running on it, and javelins. You've got to find . . . go over and put your one leg up.

RESEARCHER: Ah, hurdles, that's right, you just have to run the right way, don't you, for hurdles.

ALEX: You've got to not go on green.

RESEARCHER: Do you have to keep pressing the keys to make her run?

ALEX: No. You've got to move the letters. You've got to try and move them.

Alex plays the game, making his character run and jump the hurdles. The race takes only a few seconds. His character is not the winner this time.

RESEARCHER: So you didn't win that time. Oh dear.

ALEX: Can't run that fast. I runned faster yesterday.

RESEARCHER: Did you? Were you winning yesterday when you were doing it?

ALEX: I was running fast like this with my arm like this.

RESEARCHER: Were you? Is that the best way to do it?

ALEX: I was going like this and my arm was . . . when his arm was going up. He did run like this when his . . . was going like that and he was trying to run and he was jumping over like this – and he just wins.

Alex demonstrates how he used his arms, moving arms to and fro like a hurdler.

(Video transcript, Alex Simmonds)

Developing literacy and numeracy

In the course of playing the game, Alex encountered a series of texts involving alphabetic and numeric scripts and other forms of symbolic representation. To become literate, young children need not only to become familiar with letters and numbers but to understand more broadly the role of symbols (e.g. letters, numbers or icons) as standing for ideas, concepts and activities. Playing the game repeatedly reinforced such early literacy knowledge and skills. To access the game, Alex had to find the right website and navigate through a series of screens in order to start playing. This involved recognizing on-screen icons and text-based information. For example, to make the Denise Lewis character run and jump hurdles, the player needs to press the 'B' and 'N' keys on the computer keyboard to run and the space bar to jump hurdles. These instructions are shown on a screen before the game can be played in writing and with images of the letter keys and the space bar. It is unlikely that Alex could read the instructions in the conventional sense, but he did need to recognize that this screen provided playing instructions, to make the connection between the images of the keys and those on his own keyboard and to infer from these pictures how to play the game. He also demonstrated an awareness that letters are significant. When the researcher asked if game playing involved 'pressing keys', he contradicted this, reframing the action as 'making letters move'. The researcher, who took her own literacy skills for granted, focused on the mechanical action, but Alex's response made clear that he knew that keys had different letters on them and that it was important to be specific about which letters to select.

Once the instructions were understood or recalled, he needed to press an on-screen button coloured red and marked 'PLAY', at the bottom right-hand corner of the screen, in order to move to the game itself. All of these activities can be seen as involving some of the technical skills needed to 'read' on-screen texts.

In addition to the instructions themselves, there are other types of text fulfilling other functions. At the bottom of each screen there are menus which enable players to move between different sections of the game. There are also speed and time gauges which allow players to check how well they are doing as they race. In the background of the race scene are the kinds of texts spectators see at sporting venues, a mixture of information and advertisements. The race official communicates via speech bubbles (as the game has no sound): before 'go', the bubbles read 'marks' and 'set'.

After the race has been run, another screen shows the names of the different countries to which the competitors belong, their times in the race and points accrued. As the heptathlon proceeds, points accumulate, and players can thus calculate how many they need to gain to win. Although it seems unlikely that Alex could interpret these numbers accurately as heptathlon scores are typically four- or five-digit numbers, he was learning that scores are expressed numerically and represent the quality of the performance. The scoreboard also showed rankings (i.e. which player was in first, second or third position), and these simpler representations of player position were probably more comprehensible for a child of Alex's age. We do not know how much, if any, of this textual and numerical information Alex could understand: none of it is necessary for playing the game. But the presence of these texts, as with many other instances of environmental print in the real world, contributes to children's growing awareness of the role which texts and numbers play in our daily lives and to their desire to become literate and numerate so that they too have access to the information conveyed. Thus, in terms of early literacy, the game provides a rich environment for young children to encounter texts and to gradually uncover their role through the game's activities.

Increasing knowledge of the world

The game also contributed to Alex's knowledge of the world around him. Many children of this age become fascinated by a particular field of knowledge, such as dinosaurs. In Alex's case, his area of interest was sports. In the course of playing this game (among others on the site), he learnt a range of technical terms, such as 'heptathlon', 'hurdles' and 'javelin', which are not usually found in the vocabulary of four-year-old children. Moreover, he knew what athletes needed to do to participate in the various disciplines of the heptathlon. As can be inferred from the vignette above, he physically demonstrated to the researchers the moves required for hurdling, including very specific leg and arm movements. The game had also made him aware of the need to combine fast running with jumping the hurdles at the right moment and of the need to build up a rhythm. Games of this kind, which simulate real world activities, seem to be particularly effective at conveying the techniques of physical activity. A written text which described how to hurdle would be impenetrable for Alex and, in any case, it would probably be difficult to translate the words into physical movements. Watching hurdlers in action, live or on television, would provide more information about the physical movements, but the event would be over so quickly that the spectator would be unlikely to be able to study the moves in detail. Learning to hurdle oneself is likely to be more effective than a simulation, but at Alex's age and height (which was about the same as a standard hurdle) this was not yet a possibility.

Dispositions to learn

From the various examples we have already discussed, it will be clear that preschool children enjoy learning to use technology and learning with technology. There is satisfaction in learning new skills, particularly when these provide access to desirable activities such as watching DVDs, interacting with toys or playing games. Children are also proud to be able to do these things well and pleased with the praise their parents give them, particularly when their parents say that their children are better or faster at using various technologies than the parents are themselves. For similar reasons, children may enjoy learning some of the overtly 'educational' material presented to them by technological toys such as Leapsters or V-Tech consoles. In Scotland, as in other Western societies, learning letters, numbers, colours and shapes is expected of preschool children, and clearly valued by parents, preschool practitioners and other adults. Children are keen to please and to be praised for these kinds of achievements. Thus for most preschool children, learning to use technologies, and acquiring the skills to which they provide access, are enjoyable and satisfying experiences.

These early learning experiences in the home contribute to positive dispositions to learn in preschool and when children start school. In addition, early experiences of learning with technology appear to support other aspects of the learning process which are likely to be of value in more formal educational contexts, such as, understanding the importance of following instructions carefully or persisting with tasks which initially seem too difficult. Rory, a four-year-old boy living with his parents and two older sisters, was developing these skills as he played a Thomas the Tank Engine game on the family computer.

Rory: Learning to follow instructions

Rory was a fan of Thomas the Tank Engine. He loved the books, the toy engines and the DVDs of the television series, which he had watched repeatedly. For a Christmas present, his parents bought him a Thomas the Tank Engine game to play on the family computer along with the controller for the game, which was designed to look like the steering wheel of a steam engine. This was placed carefully – by a parent – on the computer keyboard, so that pressure exerted by a child 'steering' the wheel activated appropriate control keys. The game simulated driving around a railway track and incorporated a number of tasks, at progressively more difficult levels.

At first, Rory found the game challenging because he did not pay attention to the instructions, which were spoken aloud at the beginning of each level of the game. As a result, he had difficulty completing the tasks but because the idea of driving Thomas the Tank Engine himself was extremely attractive, he persisted. According to his mother, 'To begin with, I had to point out that he had to listen to these instructions in order to understand what to do, but he knows this now and listens to the instructions himself. He is much better at the game now. Before, he used to press buttons at random, but now he knows how it works, and he can concentrate for longer too. When he started he could only play for five minutes or so before he got frustrated, but now he could play for an hour or more and we have to tell him to stop. Sometimes his sisters try to help him, but he doesn't want them to do this. He wants to play by himself.'

(Fieldnotes and interviews, the Kinross family)

Technologies as cultural practices

In the research into children's early experiences with literacy, the importance of environmental print is now well-established (Goodman 1986; Adams 1990). Children grow up with printed texts all around them, from shop signs to cereal boxes. In the early years, they quickly become aware of the fact that such symbols have meaning, even if they do not know what it is. We can think of environmental technology in a similar way. Children are surrounded, in their homes and in the areas where they live, by many different technological items. Even without their attention being specifically drawn to this phenomenon, they are aware that technologies have a role in our daily lives by helping us cross the road, supplying bank notes, calculating the cost of shopping and enabling us to communicate with friends and relatives who are not in the immediate vicinity. Long before they are allowed to touch the buttons and screens which facilitate all of these activities, children are aware that these actions are significant.

Within the home, as we have seen, children do not have unlimited access to the technologies around them. While some, such as televisions and toys and games designed for young children, are widely accepted as appropriate for children and accessible to them, others, particularly mobile phones or laptops bought for adult use, are not made freely available. Domestic work technologies such as washing machines or microwaves may be deemed uninteresting to children or too dangerous for them to use. This does not mean that children are unaware of others' uses of these technologies or of what these technologies do. We have encountered children using old or broken technological items or toy mobile phones or laptops as props for role-play games involving 'going to school' or 'shopping'; we know that preschool children are keen to participate in family practices involving technologies even though they may not have the necessary skills to do so.

Colin: Technology as family practice

Three-year-old Colin lived with his mother, Ms Knox, and his five-year-old sister, Emma. Ms Knox had purchased the family's first computer, which included a broadband internet connection, Instant Messenger and a webcam, about a year before they took part in our study.

Ms Knox had very limited experiences before this, so she and the children were learning how to use these items together, initially with help from a more experienced relative. But the computer and the camera now played an important part in family life, enabling them to communicate with relatives living in Australia. They were in regular contact via email, exchanged photographs and spoke to each other using the webcam.

Though Colin could not read or write, he was a keen photographer. He took hundreds of photographs with the digital camera, and his sister helped him to download these onto the computer, from where some might be sent to Australia. Although he could not write, he liked to add emoticons, such as smiley faces, to the emails they sent. During the study, the Knox family went on an extended family holiday to Australia to visit these relatives. The opportunities Colin had had to communicate with them before they went meant that he had already had a chance to get to know them before the trip; and after they returned, electronic contact was even more important.

(Field notes and interviews, the Knox family)

The kinds of activities in which Colin was engaged here are the same as those of other members of his family. Unlike most of the other examples we have considered, these technological activities are not associated with typical preschooler needs or interests or catered for by age-appropriate toys or games or tools for early learning. Rather, he is being inducted into practices of value and significance to his family, including oral, visual and written communication with relatives, maintaining family bonds at a distance and commemorating his immediate family's life through photographs. He is learning both that these kinds of activities are important to his family, and also how to engage in them in ways which suit his family's modes of communication. If this were preparation for the kind of literacy that he will encounter at school, the written form might be privileged above the oral and the visual (and the emoticons might be condemned), but in his family these various means of communication are not separated or ranked, but rather selected according to ability, occasion and mood.

In this way we can see how Colin's technological experiences have ensured that he has learnt how to use the technologies and has also learnt through the technologies (which are clearly supporting early literacy and self-expression), but he has also learnt the role that technologies play in his family's life and their place in the culture of his own family and the wider community.

From all these examples, we can see that others – parents, siblings, friends and relatives – have an important role to play in determining not only what children learn, but also how they learn with technology. This is the focus of Chapter 8, which looks at how others, particularly adults, guide children's learning. The chapter compares children's experiences with technology at home to their experiences in preschool settings.

Guided interaction at home and preschool

In this chapter we extend our consideration of the ways in which young children's learning with technology can be supported at preschool and at home, drawing on the two major projects described earlier, Interplay and Entering e-Society. Research suggests that patterns of learning interactions differ across these two settings in areas such as numeracy (Aubrey, Bottle and Godfrey 2003) and literacy (Feiler 2005; Heath 1983; Tizard and Hughes 1984). As discussed in Chapter 7, there has been little research on young children's uses of technology at home to date, but we know that the patterns of use for older children differ across home and school (Kent and Facer 2004; Kerawalla and Crook 2002; Stevenson 2008). In this chapter, we summarize some of the key findings from the earlier chapters so that we can consider the similarities and differences in home and preschool, the two areas where young children spend most of their time.

To recap, the research project Interplay set out to explore how practitioners can enhance three- and four-year-old children's encounters with ICT in a preschool culture of child-initiated learning through play. It was prompted by our previous observations of children walking away from learning opportunities with ICT because the content of the activity was inappropriate or the technology's interface imposed too great a barrier. We identified the areas of learning that could be supported by ICT, and by working with practitioners in a process of guided enquiry, we established which practices constituted guided interaction and could make a difference to children's learning in the playroom context.

The aim of Entering e-Society was to investigate ways in which three- and four-year-olds were learning to use technologies in their home environment. Guided interaction was not a specific focus, although it was used as a way of analysing the support for learning provided by members of the family. The study drew on an audit of key home technologies provided by a survey conducted in the early stages, but used case studies as the main form of data collection because case studies enabled us to collect data from and about children in authentic settings. Although the focus was on the kinds of competences which children were developing with technology at home, we were also concerned with the potential impact of this on their formal educational development, both at preschool and as they entered primary education. Towards the end of the study, we therefore drew on preliminary findings to discuss the implications of our work on children's experiences with technology at home for future policy and practice in preschool and primary school with experts from across the UK.

Although there are obvious differences between domestic and preschool settings, the shared features of these sites of learning which are pertinent to the following discussion are:

- the presence of adults and children;
- the presence of digital and other technologies, and;
- technology being used while other activities were going on in close proximity.

The two sites of home and preschool are sociocultural and technological landscapes. In both environments the social relationships were potential sources of support and cultural practices were modelled and transmitted, but they were also spaces populated by technological and other objects. The following discussion draws on Table 8.1, which summarizes the similarities and differences in the ways in which young children's encounters with technologies are guided across these two settings as they relate to five key questions:

- Which technologies are available?
- Who provides support for children's learning with technology?
- What is the motivation for providing this support?
- How is the support provided?
- What types of learning are supported?

The technologies available have been described in some detail in earlier chapters and are summarized here. The focus in this chapter is on guided interaction, the key feature of which is that it involves another person who has greater competence or expertise relating to a technological device. Chapter 5 describes how interactions with technology can be guided either proximally or distally and can take a variety of forms, including speech, gesture and provision or arrangement of resources. We compare different forms of guided interaction across these sites, thinking about the areas of learning (i.e. operational, learning dispositions, knowledge and understanding of the world and cultural practices) that are supported.

Availability of technologies

There was at least one desktop computer available in each of the preschool playrooms. Access to other ICT resources varied; interactive whiteboards were

Table 8.1 Supporting young children's learning with technology at home and in preschool

	Home	Preschool
WHICH TECHNOLOGIES?	• diverse range of leisure, domestic and work technologies • some ownership of items by children • technologies used by both adults and children • higher specification • easily accessible • technology as cultural and educational resource	• selected range of technologies, with focus on computers • no ownership of items by children • technologies used by children, but rarely by adults • lower specification • time-limited access • technology as educational resource
WHO PROVIDES SUPPORT?	• inter-generational & intra-generational support • family members • adult-child and child-child • adults as learners	• inter-generational support • preschool staff • adult-child, little peer support • adults as learners
WHY IS SUPPORT PROVIDED?	• as play activity • prepare children for school and work but not always explicitly oriented to learning • allow adults time for their own activities	• as play activity • prepare children for school and work • meet demands of curriculum
HOW IS SUPPORT PROVIDED?	• support as social activity • help-seeking is uninhibited • spontaneous • guided interaction (distal): modelling, monitoring, providing resources, setting up activities • guided interaction (proximal): demonstrating, enjoying, explaining, instructing, managing, modelling, monitoring, prompting, providing feedback	• support as individual activity • help-seeking is limited • planned • guided interaction (distal): monitoring, planning, providing resources, setting up activities • guided interaction (proximal): some demonstrating, instructing, managing, but limited modelling, monitoring, prompting, providing feedback

(continued)

Table 8.1 Continued

	Home	Preschool
WHAT TYPES OF LEARNING ARE SUPPORTED?	• children determine own goals within available resources • encompasses operational, dispositions to learn, and knowledge of the world • understanding the cultural role of technologies • communication and maintenance of family relationships	• children determine own goals within available resources • mainly dispositions to learn and operational; some knowledge of the world but limited awareness of the cultural role of technologies

Source: Plowman L., Stephen C. and McPake, J. (in press). Reproduced with permission of the publisher.

being used in some settings and there was fairly widespread use of digital cameras by both adults and children to make a record of various activities. Practitioners tended to think of ICT only in terms of desktop computers, but they were encouraged by us to think about extending its range to encompass cameras, electronic keyboards and some of the toys that can be found in preschool settings. Because some of these technologies are more familiar to practitioners, they promote confidence, they can be more affordable and they can give children the opportunity to build on competences and knowledge that they may develop in the home.

Our family survey data showed that almost all of our respondents owned at least one mobile phone, while three-quarters possessed televisions with interactive features and three-quarters had computers with internet access. As we have seen in the previous chapters, a high level of technology in the home did not necessarily mean technologies were made available to the children and, where they were, it did not always mean that children were drawn to use them, even when encouraged by their families. Although almost every family owned at least one mobile phone, fewer than one in seven of the children (14 per cent) were allowed to use them alone, although almost half could use the phone if supervised. Two-thirds (66 per cent) of the children whose parents had internet access were allowed to use it, but in almost all cases (90 per cent) this was reported as with adult supervision. However, these data provided only a limited amount of information about how children use these technologies or why children may be prohibited or discouraged from using them. The case studies allowed us to explore children's experiences with technologies in greater detail and to consider what factors may lead to some children having more extensive opportunities to learn with technologies than others.

Who provides guided interaction?

The practitioners were the main source of guided interaction in preschool. We found that they had an extensive repertoire of pedagogical actions to support learning but lacked confidence in how they could apply this expertise to enhance children's encounters with ICT. Their focus on child-centred practice meant that preschool staff felt uncomfortable with behaviours that they perceived to be too directive, but the interventions developed as part of Interplay showed that it was possible to combine a child-centred approach with the targeted support needed when young children use ICT in preschool settings.

Peer support for learning was more limited than practitioners believed to be the case. Although practitioners cited collaborative use of the computer as evidence of peer support, we found that children actively helped each other infrequently. While it was fairly common for children to be sitting in front of a computer in pairs or groups, it was unusual for them to provide mutual support and peer tutoring. Their communication with each other tended to be nonverbal, and while this occasionally manifested itself as shared laughter and enjoyment, it was often the case that interaction was aimed at individuals gaining access to, or prolonging, a sought after activity. Nonverbal communication was more often a means of gaining access to or dominating use of the computer than supporting each other; the most frequently identified interactions in this situation were taking control of the mouse, moving closer to the screen when they wanted to join in and prolonging their turn by upending the sand timer which was used to time sessions.

Our interviews and observations suggested that the sources of guided interaction at home were more diverse than in the nursery, including parents and other adult relatives, family friends and older siblings and cousins. One of the research activities was designed to probe the children's perspective on learning to use technology. They were presented with a picture of a child and were asked to tell us how easy or difficult it would be for 'Ben' or 'Lucy' to learn how to use each of three or four pictured items, and who they could ask for help. Not every child was able to understand this exercise, but children were only presented with pictures of items with which we knew they played and there was a high degree of recognition. Games on children's websites were generally considered to be easy to use, although some children commented that parents were needed to switch on the computer or to access the sites. In cases where items were considered to be difficult, it was usually operational skills, such as knowing which button to press or how to switch something on, that were identified as hurdles. Some children nominated themselves to help Ben or Lucy, but parents were most often cited as a source of help, followed by brothers and sisters. The child's preschool was not considered to be a source of learning with technology by the children or their parents.

The case studies revealed that a wide variety of people were supporting learning in the home, sometimes simply by being engaged in their own activities. Children could see adults going online to order shopping or book a holiday, recording family occasions with a digital video camera or using a wide range of leisure technologies. Older siblings were making calls, texting or taking photos with their mobile phones, chatting on MSN, using games consoles and downloading music. These were all authentic activities inasmuch as there was a genuine reason for getting involved in them. Sometimes children were explicitly shown how to use these technologies, but more frequently these were mundane, day-to-day activities that formed a backdrop to children's lives.

Family members bought children LeapPads, VTech Smile games consoles, portable DVD players and other technological items as Christmas and birthday presents, and showed the child how to use them. Providers of gifts, such as grandparents, neighbours, aunts or uncles, were motivated to offer support so that the recipient could enjoy playing with the item, but they did not need to be a high user of technology to do this; having time available to tutor children was more important than expertise. These benefactors would demonstrate how to use the various items, but they would also offer verbal explanations, something we saw rarely in preschool. Older siblings were also key providers of guided interaction, but as their expertise often stemmed from being high users of the computer and games consoles, they could also act as inhibitors of learning by dominating use of the technology and preventing their younger brothers and sisters from gaining access. For some children, however, cousins and siblings were an important source of hand-me-down games consoles and software as well as skills.

How is guided interaction provided?

The prevalence of guided interaction and the forms it took varied from one setting to another. Helpers at home, whether children or adults, felt fewer inhibitions than practitioners about being teacherly, and family members were able to invest time in explicit tutoring in the expectation of the child's sub-sequent independent play providing a pay-off. This tutoring tended to be targeted towards different operational skills, but otherwise children were believed to 'just pick it up' or to teach themselves, as both Ellie's mum and Cameron's mum commented in Chapter 6. As in the preschool settings, this form of guided interaction took place in the proximal dimension because explaining and demonstrating technical skills and interpreting rules and instruc-tions required face-to-face interaction at the site of engagement. However, the adult–child ratio in the nursery meant that practitioners were not generally able to provide the same level of one-to-one support.

Prior to the interventions introduced as part of the Interplay project, the most common form of support in preschools was reactive supervision, an approach which operated by default rather than constituting a pedagogical strategy. This reactive supervision was associated with free play, in which children chose for themselves when or if they would use the computer and what they would do. In these circumstances, supervision was most commonly manifested as keeping a check on taking turns and the length of time at the computer or was a reaction to the occasional requests for help when children got stuck. Language was not a dominant mode of communication for learning and the lack of extended dialogue was particularly noticeable when at the computer; children rarely initiated talk, and this remained the same whether in a group of children or with an adult. The focus on the screen inhibited communication as it made eye contact between group members difficult and the usual rules of verbal turn taking could be disrupted by the intrusion of the audio track on the computer game. During the period in which practitioners implemented their chosen interventions, we used guided enquiry to support our analysis of pedagogical interactions and noted that proximal guided interaction could be manifested as an adult placing their hand over a child's hand on the mouse, providing emotional support by sharing successes and problems, directing a child's attention by pointing or sequencing and breaking down activities. These same forms of guided interaction were demonstrated in the home, but they were part of the usual flow of family activities and could generally be provided by a greater range of people.

Many parents encouraged their children to develop operational skills so that they could use technologies for learning purposes or for enjoyment. About half of the parents had provided explicit help to show children how to set up the computer and the television, and they also said that they helped to identify and access websites, view photos on a mobile phone or take pictures with a digital camera. Used by more than two-thirds of the children at the start of the study, televisions and DVD players functioned as an entry activity. In terms of content, televisions were perceived to be less risky than the internet for unsupervised viewing at the times when children had access, as well as easy to use once set up. However, channel selection could be complex in the majority of households which had interactive television with a subscription to satellite or cable services, particularly if a DVD or video player was connected, as it necessitated use of the remote control and recognition of symbols and numbers. Parents did not want to risk the settings being altered in such a way that they could not easily be retrieved, so time was well spent tutoring children.

These technologies also provided maximum return on the adult investment in proximal guided interaction because children could occupy themselves without disturbing parents from domestic tasks and leisure activities or interrupting older siblings' play. In addition to encouraging independent use, the motivation for this tutoring was based on safety concerns as the need for an electricity supply meant that televisions and computers were potentially more hazardous than battery-operated equipment. Distal guided interaction in the form of peripheral vision was often used for overseeing safety and ensuring that children were not getting stuck, but help-seeking behaviours were more overt in the home: children were uninhibited about going to find somebody or calling for help when it was needed and family members had an incentive to be responsive to these calls for help if it prolonged the time that children could be engaged in an unsupervised activity. No clear-cut gender divide was reported in terms of provision of guided interaction by mothers and fathers, although it should be noted that lone mothers accounted for seven of the 24 households and that, in most cases, our data are based on interviews with the mothers. As they tended to spend longer periods at home, mothers were more likely to keep an eye on activities from afar, but both parents reported being equally interested in encouraging independent use and providing access to resources.

What types of learning were supported?

The children in our studies had typically acquired basic levels of competence in all three areas of learning identified in our preschool study – extending knowledge of the world, acquiring operational skills and developing dispositions to learn – by the time they were ready to start school. Interviews with practitioners and observation in the field suggested that the degree of competence children acquired across these categories depended on a number of factors including developmental stage, their own interests and preferences, access to ICT, the quality of guided interaction and the particular interests and aptitudes of practitioners as well as experiences at home.

Young children acquired operational competence at home and in the playroom, although the emphasis in preschool settings was generally on computers, while in the home this was supplemented by televisions, DVD players, technological toys, mobile phones and games consoles. Children's learning at home meant that they could switch items on and off and rewind and fast forward. They also understood that digital technologies could be used to communicate with friends and relatives, by phone (voice, texting and picture messaging), by email and, in a few cases, by webcam. The reliance on computer software in preschool meant learning was more limited in scope, with an emphasis on operations, but once practitioners explored alternative technologies through the guided enquiry interventions, their evidence about children's learning was heavily weighted towards developing dispositions to learn. Parents were more likely to focus on children's operational skills when tutoring was intentional, but otherwise tended to underestimate their role in supporting skills such as changing television channels, pausing a DVD or sending a text message because these things seemed unremarkable.

As it became apparent during the course of the case studies that some parents found it difficult to conceptualize their children's activities as learning, we found a fruitful approach was to ask 'Has your child done anything with technology since our last visit that you didn't realize they could do?' All parents responded with examples, including children rewinding a video in slow motion, locating cable television channels, resizing a window on a website and using digital cameras or a laptop's trackpad in a controlled manner. Some parents commented on their children's use of terminology and reported children using words such as 'pause', 'desktop' and 'load', demonstrating awareness of web addresses on television programmes or asking for a site to be saved in 'Favourites'.

Family settings also afforded opportunities to develop dispositions that promoted learning, including sustained attention, following instructions and routines, problem-solving skills and exploration. Children added to their knowledge of the world at home as they did in the playroom, as many children were using technologies to support the development of early literacy and numeracy or, occasionally, to find information on the web, although neither parents nor practitioners paid particular attention to the learning that might be described as subject content.

In our research in children's homes we identified an area of learning which we referred to as learning about technologies as cultural practices. We defined this as children's understanding of the roles which technology plays for a range of social and cultural purposes, such as communication, work, self-expression or entertainment. The description of guided interaction provided earlier in this book was based on fieldwork in preschools and as we did not find sufficient examples of learning about technologies as cultural practices to warrant this category it was subsumed into knowledge of the world, along with knowledge about living things and places. However, the domestic context offered more opportunities to develop an awareness of these cultural practices than preschool settings, and the interviews with parents, conversations with children and observations led us to return to this category and elaborate our understanding of it. This is therefore an additional area of learning to which the home is the major contributor. It includes children's understanding of the roles which technology plays in family life and in the wider world, and their ability to harness this understanding for a range of social and cultural purposes.

Over the lifetime of the project, families acquired different technologies for different purposes. The children were thus being inducted into various cultural practices ranging from talking to relatives on mobile phones to taking and printing digital photos of the family pets, sharing memories by watching family video recordings of special events and using discarded computers and non-functioning mobile phones as props for play in imaginary offices, shops and schools. Children demonstrated to parents that they understood that technologies could be used to communicate with friends and relatives, even if they were not able to use all of these modes of communication unassisted. Parents tended to be unaware of their role in introducing children to cultural practices with technologies, in part because the culture in which they lived was not visible to them – it was just the way things were.

Sites of learning: home and preschool

Our analysis suggests some key differences in the home and preschool as learning environments, as summarized in Table 8.1. The contrast is not as simplistic as a distinction between formal and informal learning because preschool education is predicated on learning through play, which is seen as a natural activity for children of this age and does not need to be site-specific. Furthermore, instruction is usually associated with formal educational settings but, as we have seen, it was more likely to take place in the informal setting of the home than the preschool.

Different metaphors for the gap between out-of-school and school as sites of learning have been used by researchers examining the integration of knowledge developed in these different settings, particularly in terms of literacy practices. Gregory (2005), for instance, refers to 'interspace' to describe the ways in which school discourse may be taken home and transformed into home talk through play, but Gregory also stresses the importance of teachers recognizing children's different linguistic and cultural resources in their classroom practices and provision. Others (Gutiérrez, Baquedano-Lopez and Tejeda 2000) have enrolled the metaphor of 'third space' to describe the integration of knowledge from the different spaces of home and school.

In her discussion of literacy practices at home and school, Marsh (2003: 273) suggests that there was more evidence of the nursery infiltrating the home than vice versa. While her observation that 'literacy practices are inextricably linked to geographical space' refers to what we might call traditional literacies of reading and writing, it is clear that opportunities to support and develop children's learning with and through technology, including their emerging digital literacies, also differ across home and preschool. Marsh's (op. cit.) metaphor of 'one-way traffic' refers to the ways in which the dominant con-ceptualization of literacy is derived from the school and nursery and permeates parents' perceptions of the value of their family practices. In our case, this was seen in parents' lack of awareness of the learning that could develop as a result of their children observing the ways in which family members used technologies. Instead, they focused on the more visible operational skills, such as using a mouse, with which nurseries were more preoccupied. Nevertheless, the report of one parent that she had been told by a teacher that children would be shown how to use the keyboard and mouse 'properly' at school is an indication of the disregard for competences and dispositions acquired at home.

Our research suggests that young children acquire a wide range of compe-tences when interacting with technology in the home, but these were developed in ways which were not necessarily the result of direct teaching. Learning with and through technologies at home can be characterized as authentic, taking place on a need-to-know basis and when required, having a favourable ratio of potential tutors to children and providing opportunities for children to 'pick up' their learning. Children's experiences at home introduced them to the use of technology for communication, self-expression, work-related tasks and entertainment, and so began to prepare children for a life in which technology would play an important role.

The facilitators for the child's learning at home included interactions between resources from the social landscape of the home (i.e. grandparents, other relatives, family friends, older siblings and parents) and resources from the technological landscape, the environmental technology to which we referred in Chapter 7. Children's learning took place as a result of trial and error, observation and copying, in addition to demonstration by more able others, and their individual preferences, interests and dispositions were important influences on the activities they chose. Parents expressed the belief that children's competences with technology were mainly the result of being self-taught and they were unaware of the ways in which they supported their child's learning by modelling uses of technology and providing opportunities to participate in and observe authentic activities.

Table 8.1 shows that, while there are a number of commonalities across the two sites, there are key differences. In the distal dimension there are similarities in terms of provision of resources and setting up activities, although modelling is more prevalent in the home and is provided by both adults and other children. In the proximal dimension there is more explicit and contingent instruction and demonstration at home because the adult–child ratio is more favourable for these activities and proximal interactions are more readily supported when it is easy to identify if a child needs help.

Developing practice

Our analysis of children's learning with technology at home suggests that the broader range of technologies available there, combined with more potential helpers, led to a wider range of learning opportunities. It is therefore worth considering which aspects of learning with and through technology in the home could inform the development of practice.

If nursery settings were able to support learning with ICT by providing a wider range of technologies, by encouraging a sense of ownership and by providing a wider variety of forms of guided interaction, we would find the 'traffic' to which Marsh alludes (op. cit.) going in the other direction. This is not to suggest that the ways in which young children learn at home should be used as a model for practice in the nursery unquestioningly. The preschool playroom is designed primarily as a space for education, so it is not surprising that it is distinct from the home in many ways, not only in how children interact with technologies or in the authenticity of activities. Nevertheless, given our descriptions of how children learn with technology at home, it is worth thinking about what would constitute authentic tasks in the preschool environment and whether there is scope to develop pedagogy and practice to develop features of home learning that are applicable in the nursery.

There were few examples of using technology for real-life activities in preschool settings as practitioners used the computer sited in the separate office for activities such as producing letters to go home or printing photographs and posters. As this was out of sight of the children, occasions for modelling uses of ICT and providing opportunities for children to learn the cultural and social value of technology were restricted. Interactive whiteboards were found in some preschool settings, but these are explicitly an educational resource not found in homes or used for other purposes. In the home, authentic activities were commonplace and a richer range of technologies for study, work and leisure was available, typically with higher specifications than would be usual in the playroom. In these cases, guided interaction was incidental rather than explicit. It was clear that parents and practitioners overlooked the potential of children's legitimate peripheral participation as a way of learning, but the activities and the technologies need to be visible and have genuine applications for children to benefit in this way. The technological landscape of the home meant that children were constantly aware of its environmental technology and so there were many opportunities for children to interact with or observe family members, creating a link between family culture and children's learning.

Although parents invested some time in tutoring, their children developed a wide range of competences by 'picking it up'. This is compatible with the free play ethos of the nursery because rather than direct instruction it benefits from the ways in which children learn how to do things by observing others who have greater expertise, a process of learning known as 'legitimate peripheral participation' (Lave and Wenger 1991). This practice happened by default in the home and was an effective way for children to develop all four forms of learning that we have described. Greater awareness of the potential for learning through legitimate peripheral participation could lead to changes in practice so that children can be offered more opportunities to engage in authentic activities of the kind found in the home. This approach would be sympathetic to practitioners' concerns about being teacherly, but would necessitate placing technologies used for day-to-day tasks in a more visible location in the play-room. If practitioners asked parents about the competences 'picked up' by their children at home, it might also increase parents' awareness of this learning and the value they attach to it.

Practitioners had ways of informing parents about their children's activities at the nursery, but the preschool was not seen by parents or children as a source of learning about or with technology. Other than some examples of children taking home digital photographs of the day's activities to show their parents, we found no examples of technology being used to engineer cross-domain learning in the way that story sacks or shoeboxes can be used to develop literacy. Practitioners had a restricted view of what children could do, and therefore of how they could develop their learning, because children did not have opportunities to demonstrate the competences developed at home on the more limited range of technologies and activities in the nursery. However, parents were not necessarily aware of what their children could do either: some were surprised by their children's knowledge or competences and used 'just picking it up' as a way of making sense of this learning.

This is not to promote a hands-off approach to learning with and through technology; some of the problems inherent in such an approach, such as boredom, frustration and a lack of sustained attention, were illustrated in Chapter 5. Rather, it is to consider guided interaction in its entirety as a way of thinking about support for learning. This means including support for the operational learning that we know is necessary, as well as using different modes of support which are enacted both proximally and distally for cultural awareness, knowledge and understanding and developing learning dispositions. Increasing the number of potential adult helpers is not a feasible solution for most nurseries, but we have demonstrated that having a richer mix of technologies in the playroom can bring many benefits.

While desktop computers have a place, selecting resources that do not have their high supervision overhead and which are more likely to lend themselves to peer learning can lead to richer learning experiences. In many cases, these will be the same technologies found in domestic settings, such as digital still and video cameras, portable DVD players, MP3 players and electronic keyboards, as well as games consoles and other electronic toys designed for young children, such as microwave ovens and cash registers. Discarded items from home, such as mobile phones, baby monitors and laptop computers can be used for role play. Children can also be given opportunities to interact with the technologies which are in daily use by the nursery staff but which tend to be located out of sight, such as scanners and printers. In addition to the environmental technologies in the home, children can also explore everyday uses of technology in their local environment, such as traffic lights, cash machines and supermarket scanning devices.

Although we have suggested that technologically-mediated interactions in preschool settings were impoverished by comparison with what was available in many domestic settings, we observed practitioners making sensitive and contingent responses when children were engaged in playroom activities such as baking or completing jigsaw puzzles. The interactions necessary to support children's learning with ICT in the playroom were therefore already present in the practitioner's repertoire, but these aspects of practice were not frequently observed when children played with technology. As described at greater length in Chapter 4, there were several possible explanations. Making time for one-to-one interactions was not always achievable and the recourse to reactive supervision was an understandable response as practitioners typically had oversight of more than one activity. The process of casting an eye over the room to monitor play and levels of engagement does not reveal problems at the computer screen and a child walking away from an unproductive encounter with ICT may not be noticed if they settle readily in a different activity. These problems could be compounded by practitioners' lack of confidence with some technologies.

Another explanation was found in the practitioners' understanding of their role. Exploration is the favoured mode of learning in nurseries, unlike school classrooms, and the element of guidance in guided interaction can be interpreted as too prescriptive. Practitioners' implicit theory of practice rests on a Piagetian concept of learning that fits with their desire for child-led playroom experiences and emphasizes their role as providers and facilitators but tends to underplay the value of their direct interactions with children. However, our evidence argues not for a shift to didacticism, but for mindful interactions that are sensitive to the context and to individual needs. This is in line with findings from a large-scale study (Sylva, Taggart, Siraj-Blatchford, Totsika, Ereky-Stevens, Gilden and Bell 2007: 53) which defined effective pedagogy in the playroom as focusing 'on planned interactions and extending child-initiated activities in a purposefully designed learning context rather than merely reacting to spontaneous activities in an unthought-of or ad hoc manner'. This interpretation of effective pedagogy, like our analysis of guided interaction, extends, rather than replaces, free play and does not privilege formal instruction.

Chapter 9

Young children learning in a digital age

Children born at the start of the twenty-first century are growing up in a world in which digital technologies are not only widely accessible to most families living in Western societies, but so commonplace as to be unremarkable. Although their parents can remember times before computers, games consoles, mobile phones or interactive toys were in everyday use, for many preschool children in the first decade of the century, these are as much a part of the furniture of the home as washing machines, televisions and stereo music systems – the 'new' technologies popularized by previous generations.

In their early years, children learn to use these by watching others, by trying things out themselves when they are ready and by wanting to be able to do the kinds of things which these technologies offer, including entertainment, opportunities to learn, ways of communicating with others and forms of self-expression. These kinds of activities are interwoven with other typical childhood pastimes: playing outside, helping to cook, chatting to friends, going shopping, reading stories, dancing, singing and tidying up. While some adults find it surprising that children pick up the skills needed to use technological items without seeming to need tuition, for the children themselves, the demands of using a television remote control, a mouse or on-screen instructions are not necessarily more (or less) of a challenge than other tasks they need to master: getting dressed, tying shoelaces, using a pencil, learning the shapes of letters and numbers and crossing the road safely. All of these skills are learnt by a mixture of instruction, observation and practice and because they are the kinds of skills they need in their daily lives.

We set out to answer some key questions posed by those involved in the upbringing of young children. We conclude by returning to some questions posed in Chapter 1:

- Is it important for children of this age to learn to use technology?
- Are some children in a better position than others to take advantage of technology?
- Which technologies are best suited to their needs?

- How can preschool practitioners recognize and extend children's experiences with technology?

This chapter summarizes our answers to these questions, discussed at length over the course of this book, with a particular focus on the transition to school and the policy implications of our conclusions.

Is it important for children of this age to learn to use technology?

When we asked parents this question, the answers we received varied. Many parents were convinced of the importance of technological skills, in particular those associated with using computers, in their children's future lives. Some focused on their use in educational contexts, but a more common response was to comment that many jobs currently require people to be familiar with electronic communications of various kinds, and that this trend was likely to be even more pronounced by the time their children had grown up. For these parents, becoming familiar with technology at an early age and feeling confident about using different types of equipment was valuable preparation. There was a risk that their children would miss out in future, either at school or at work, if they failed to become confident users of technologies while they were young. For some parents, however, such benefits were questionable; aware that the technological landscape had changed dramatically over the last decade and, in some cases, that skills they themselves had acquired in earlier times were now obsolete, they were sceptical as to whether early familiarity with technology would be of particular value. These parents believed that their children would acquire the skills they needed at the appropriate time. This perception was often accompanied by a view that other activities (e.g. playing outside and with friends, engaging in artistic activities and learning to read, write and count) were more appropriate for the early years. For these parents, the issue was about what aspects of childhood their children would miss out on if they spent time on technological activities now.

Practitioners similarly found it difficult to determine the place of technological activity in the nursery and how this should relate to other aspects of the early years curriculum. Partly, this was because they tended to have a relatively narrow definition of what constituted technological activity, focusing principally on computers, but it was also because they were often lacking in confidence about their own technological abilities. Most of the preschool settings we visited in the course of our research had separated the technological activities in which the practitioners themselves engaged (i.e. emailing, printing and downloading photographs) from the playroom, with the result that children rarely saw or participated in adult technological practices. This was very different from their home experiences, where most children were aware of the ways in which their parents, older siblings and other family friends and relatives made use of technology, even if they themselves were not always able to take part at this stage. For this reason, practitioners tended to focus on overtly educational gains to be made: the acquisition of basic operational skills, certain learning dispositions, such as taking turns, and the educational content of the activity facilitated by the technology. All of these could be seen as having a certain value, but, apart from the operational skills, could be achieved by other means.

Although our research has not focused in detail on the expectations of teachers in primary schools, there is evidence that they too tend to focus on operational skills and on the use of technology to support learning in other areas of the curriculum and that they are largely unaware of the nature or extent of experiences with technology that many children will have had by the time they start school. None of the parents with a child moving to school during our studies reported being asked about their child's use of technologies at home, nor was there any discussion about what kinds of technological activity the children would be likely to encounter when they started school.

Towards the end of our research for Entering e-Society, in 2007, we convened an experts' forum with participants from the UK inspectorates, preschool settings, local authorities and curriculum agencies. The aim was to discuss current perspectives on the use of ICT in preschool playrooms and the early years of primary school, and the implications of the research for future policy and practice. The experts confirmed the emphasis on operational skills in the first year of primary school (age five) and believed that both children and parents could be disappointed at the impoverished range of technologies available there. They considered that few schools are currently in a position to build on the well-developed competences which many children have already acquired by the time they start formal schooling. They acknowledged that staff in primary schools might be judgemental about children's practices at home, and know little about them, and parallels were drawn with a time when teachers believed that parents should not teach their children to read and write because that was the job of the school. Now that policy has begun to take more account of prior learning and moved on from the concept of a new start on transition to primary school, the experts felt this should extend to the development of children's competences with ICT at home. The discussion reflected the views of Ackerman and Barnett (2005): it may be more meaningful to think in terms of whether schools are ready for children than whether children are ready for school.

These findings indicate that parental intuitions around this question – that the early acquisition of technological skills will have more bearing on their children's future careers and their adult lives in general than on their school education – are accurate, for the moment, at least. As far as their children's progress at school is concerned, learning to use technologies at an early age is not particularly valuable because preschool and primary practitioners do not fully recognize or build on the competences children have already acquired.

In fact, it is not difficult for children who have had limited opportunities to use technologies at home to catch up with their more technologically-experienced peers, at least in terms of the basic skills looked for by the school. However, many parents thought that their children would need technological skills, confidence with different types of technology and an awareness of the ways in which different technologies can be used for work purposes when they left school and started looking for work.

Are some children in a better position than others to take advantage of technology?

One of the motivations for our research into children's experiences with technology at home was to establish whether children from less affluent backgrounds might be at a disadvantage compared with children from more affluent backgrounds. This reflected extensive debate over the last decade concerning digital divides – the notion that certain sectors of the population might have less access and fewer opportunities to make use of technologies than others. Some of the data we collected confirmed that a family's financial position could make a difference, particularly in terms of internet access, which was more prevalent among affluent families participating in our surveys than among those with little money. However, our case studies showed that access issues for children are more complex than this. Wealthy families where parents owned expensive technological equipment for their own work or domestic purposes might restrict children's access to this equipment precisely because it was expensive and might easily be damaged. Families with little money were often resourceful about acquiring technologies second-hand. The equipment might be older and less sophisticated, but this could mean that it was more straightforward for children to use and that there was less concern about damage.

More significant indicators of the opportunities children were likely to be given to use technologies at home were their parents' past experiences and their parents' views on the future usefulness of these experiences. Parents who were competent users of technology themselves and who had a positive view of the value of technological skills were more likely to introduce their children to technologies and support their learning than parents who had limited skills or were less convinced that this was important (sometimes as a result of negative experiences they had with technology in the past). Some parents in the latter category were swayed by arguments that playing computer games or spending time on the internet was detrimental to young children, depriving them of the benefits of more traditional activities such as physical, imaginative and creative play and social engagement with other children.

We also found that children's own preferences had an important part to play. Some children growing up in families with technologically enthusiastic and supportive parents and a range of different technological items at their disposal were simply uninterested in the kinds of activities to which the technologies provided access. Others, in families with less equipment and a more ambivalent attitude, learnt to use the technological items that interested them in other places – typically at the homes of friends or relatives – and successfully persuaded their parents to buy the equipment they wanted.

As a result, the children in our studies were starting school with different kinds of technological competences. Most had basic operational skills: they could use remote controls and other push-button controllers. Many were familiar with icons and on-screen menus, though their ability to use these with ease tended to be limited by their as yet very basic literacy skills. Depending on the kinds of technology available in their homes, their opportunities to observe others using them and also to participate in these activities themselves, their experiences of technologies as support for communication, learning, domestic work, creative activities or entertainment were likely to be quite varied. But, as we have seen, the extent to which any of them might be able to build on their existing knowledge and expertise, whatever it consisted of, was likely to be quite limited.

Which technologies are best suited to the needs of young children?

The conclusion we draw from our research is that, both in the home and in preschool settings, children are most likely to develop competences that are relevant to them in contexts where technologies are integrated with the environment and recognized as having a useful role to play, rather than treated as in some way different or special compared with other tools in use. We have seen that this approach is more likely in the home than in preschool, partly because homes are environments which have to cater for the needs of all family members and so children have greater opportunities to observe others using technologies for their own purposes. In the home context, children can learn to use technologies at times when this seems appropriate and feasible and for purposes that the child identifies as relevant. Although children may, fleetingly, have an interest in pushing buttons simply for the sake of seeing what happens – and many simple technological toys are based on this premise – their main interest in a television remote control is not button pressing per se, but rather a desire to choose their own television programmes or DVDs and to watch them when they please and as many times as they want. Thus in the home, the development of operational skills is inextricably linked with an understanding of what the technology facilitates.

In formal educational settings, recognition of the greater purpose is not always explicit. The development of operational skills can be seen as the main goal of engaging children in technological activities. The lack of interest or frustration which children sometimes experience may be because they neither know nor care why they should acquire these skills. It is certainly the case that some technological items are more accessible to young children than others.

We have seen that desktop computers are particularly difficult for children to use because, in terms of both their physical construction and their interface, they are designed for bigger, more literate people. However, technological items specifically designed for young children often lack elements that can make adult technologies seem more attractive to them. For example, although children's consoles are designed for small hands and emerging literacy, the games on offer are usually educational tasks disguised as entertainment: the 'magic' pen which reads a book aloud one word at a time, providing you have the dexterity and patience to point to them in sequence, is meant to support the development of early word recognition skills rather than the pleasure of hearing a story read aloud; the 'games' which involve counting or simple sums are less engaging than those where you can complete heroic missions in the persona of your favourite television or film character. There is a need on the part of manufacturers to recognize that though young children may still be developing their motor skills and are in the early stages of becoming literate, their interests are often much more wide ranging and ambitious than the kinds of activities that children's technologies currently permit.

How can preschool practitioners recognize and extend children's experiences with technology?

Our work with preschool practitioners has shown that when it is accepted that technological items are part of the playroom environment, and that activities which involve technologies should be framed, included and supported in the same way as others such as baking or role play games, it is easier for practitioners to apply the principles of guided interaction which they already use in other contexts. This may mean, first of all, greater attention to the distal aspect of guided interaction than may typically be the case when thinking about technologies. What scenarios within the playroom would allow children to see technologies as part of daily life? Would it be useful to enable them to observe practitioners using technologies for their administrative work? Would it be a good idea to build more technological opportunities into the 'home', the 'shop' or the 'school' corners or other role-play scenarios, so that the different technological tools available in the playroom are incorporated in real-life settings?

In order to incorporate technologies as part of cultural practice in the playroom, practitioners need to understand how children experience them in the home context. This means both developing existing mechanisms to support links between home and school so that they systematically include discussion about technological interests and activities and identifying ways in which the preschool setting can build on these.

Moving from preschool to school

Practitioners are encouraged to value home learning, but the lack of research in this area has meant that it has not been possible so far to be more specific about the nature of children's experiences with technology at home or the ways in which they might inform practice. This book has identified a number of areas for consideration in the development of policy in this area or in planning for initial teacher education, vocational training for nursery staff and professional development courses. These areas include acknowledging the range and diversity of children's early experiences and developing a broader vision of the nature of children's existing technological competences. The limitations on the technologies available in most preschool settings and the lack of use by staff meant that children's awareness of the different cultural and work-related uses of technology was restricted. Children may not have been able to operate some of the technologies they saw in use at home, but they had an awareness of their function because the activities were culturally embedded in family members' day-to-day lives. In addition to this learning about technology as cultural practice, children developed diverse operational competences and learning dispositions at home. Even in households with relatively limited access to technology, the home provided a much richer mix than many preschool settings, as well as providing opportunities for children to observe and participate in authentic activities. Our findings suggest that currently preschool and primary staff have limited knowledge of children's home experiences with technology, so they are not in a position to optimize this learning. Moreover, the kinds of ICT-related skills which primary school teachers choose to develop in their pupils have little in common with the competences that children develop at home. Understanding children's experiences across the different contexts of home and preschool enables us to identify ways in which their prior learning can be supported. If schools are able to recognize and build on the wide range of competences and dispositions children bring from home and from preschool education, they will be better able to support children's learning in ways that have implications for their future, increasingly technologized education.

We introduced two of our case-study children, Evie MacGregor and Andy Kerr, both aged four, in the Introduction to this book. Evie's favourite plaything at the time was her LeapPad and, although her parents had a computer, they had no internet access. Her parents had some anxieties about the computer and could not really see its value, so Evie was not allowed to use it. This was partly because they were worried about damage, partly because both she and her parents preferred more traditional activities and partly because of health concerns. Evie was to start primary school in the village that August. It was a very small, rural school with plenty of computers. The MacGregors thought that these were used largely by the older children and that Evie was unlikely to use them.

Andy liked his Game Boy, had a number of computer games on CD-ROM and played others on children's websites. He often shared activities at the computer, which had broadband access, with his dad, and they would look up websites for the programmes he liked watching on the television. The Kerrs encouraged this because they thought it was important for his future that he felt confident with the computer. Andy also liked football, swimming and playing on his bike with friends. Although his mother did not use the computer for much other than the odd email, his father sometimes used it to work from home, edit photographs and bank and shop online. Andy was also to start primary school after the summer, at a fairly large school in town. There would be three computers in his classroom, although he did not seem particularly interested in this as he has not been very impressed by the computer in his nursery.

We visited Evie and Andy again, several months later, after they had started at primary school. In the Conclusion, we return to find out about their experiences there.

Conclusion

Starting school

Evie, age four and a half

At the age of four and a half, Evie started attending the small primary school in the village where she and her parents lived. Altogether, the school had 18 pupils, aged between four and ten. They were taught in two classrooms: one for the first three years of primary education (P1 to P3, ages five to seven) and one for the next four years (P4 to P7, ages eight to eleven), after which the children transferred to secondary school.

The school played an important place in the life of the village: its playground was open to all the village children after school hours and social events were held there regularly. In the summer before she started school, Evie and her parents were invited to a school barbecue so that they could meet the other parents and children. They also had a more formal induction visit where they saw Evie's classroom, one of the two in this small school. They met the teacher and the other children in the class, and had an introduction to the curriculum for the first year of primary school. Evie focused on the fact that they would do a lot of drawing and painting, while her Mum reminded her that she would be learning reading, writing and numbers as well.

Evie's classroom had three desktop computers and the school also had a set of laptops shared between the two classes. The school's handbook described a policy of introducing ICT from P1 but the role of classroom technology was seen as principally serving other subject areas, through programmes supporting literacy and numeracy in particular. Children were also to be taught word-processing skills, though it was stressed that this would not diminish the importance of good handwriting. Mrs MacGregor was impressed by the amount of technology available in such a small school, but thought that the younger children would not use them for school work: 'They won't actually do their work on them,' she reported, 'but they might get to use them after they have finished the work for the day, as a reward.'

Just before Evie started school, her parents signed up for an internet package. 'It's changed our lives in ways we didn't expect at all,' Mrs MacGregor told us. 'We use it every day, even if it's just to check email. I'm doing all my shopping online now, because it's cheaper and they deliver to the house. And you can find more interesting and unique stuff than in the high street.'

Evie was also using the internet on a regular basis, visiting sites linked to her favourite television programmes. She had stopped playing with the LeapPad because she now felt it was babyish in comparison to the websites. Her parents were pleased that she could play web-based games without needing supervision. 'I'm not surprised by this,' said her Mum, 'because she's always been very quick. She picked it up very fast – if we set her up on one website, quite often we'll come back and find she's playing something quite different.' At that time her parents could control the amount of time she spent on the computer because Evie did not know how to switch it on or how to access the internet. They were reluctant to teach her these skills because that would mean that she would be completely independent of them and they would no longer be able to keep track of what she was doing.

Life changed in other ways when Evie started school. She had homework to do, both reading and number work, and this limited her time for play. She was becoming more interested in books, and would try to read them herself, working out the words and asking her parents for help when she could not do this herself. She was picking these things up very quickly, even though she was the youngest in the school. Her parents thought that the preparation they had done with her before school started had helped. 'We've always encouraged her to be interested in stories – she loves her books. The LeapPad didn't really help her to learn to read and write. It was more through reading stories and being talked to. She is very intelligent.' They were pleased that the school stressed grammar and punctuation from the start, 'even at such a young age.'

Their view that it was not necessary to prepare Evie for learning with technology at school seemed to be borne out by their early experiences. 'The school doesn't expect it. Perhaps the older ones are expected to use more technology, but not the wee ones. I don't think anything she does at home is relevant to what she's learning at school.' But they did think that understanding technology would be useful to her when she left school. 'It's not really something they need to learn for school, but the more Evie learns to use these things, the more of an advantage she'll have when she leaves school. It will help her find a job.'

Andy, age five

Andy was five years old when he moved from the nursery class to P1 in the same school building. The school had just over 400 pupils, and Andy joined 28 other children in one of the two P1 classes for five-year-olds. Before he started school, his nursery had helped to prepare children for the transition by setting up a school corner and doing some literacy and numeracy work using Letterland, a reading scheme, and Numberlies, a preschool counting programme, as preparation. Andy had been assigned a buddy, a ten-year-old pupil in P6 who would help him find his way around at the beginning of the year. Nursery children had already attended some school assemblies and also used the school gym on occasion, so were familiar with the building. Andy was excited about being able to play in the 'big' playground where children from five to seven years old play. In the summer term, he and the other children who would be starting in P1 spent a morning in their new classroom. There were three computers there, but there was no discussion of the purposes for which these might be used.

The school handbook stressed the school's commitment to ICT, particularly as a way of providing information and storytelling. Each class was equipped with a listening centre as well as access to radio, television, video and computers. Pupils would have opportunities to acquire operational skills – specifically, 'use of keyboard and mouse, saving, retrieving and editing work, compiling databases, etc.' – and to use these skills across the curriculum. Younger children were not allowed to use email or the internet, but in the fourth year, after having been taught about the ethics of internet use and safety procedures, these would be introduced.

At home, Andy's parents had encouraged him to talk about starting school, but this was not a subject Andy wanted to discuss, so they had left most of the preparation to the nursery. They were pleased that the nursery had introduced reading and counting as they had been trying to interest him in books at home without much success until then. 'I just got into it myself,' Andy said.

Starting school did not diminish Andy's interest in technology. The family had acquired a laptop and Andy had learnt to use this as well as the desktop computer. He had moved on from web-based games on CBeebies to video games tied into films, such as *Cars* and *Star Wars Lego*. Mrs Kerr disapproved of the fighting elements in *Star Wars Lego* but felt that it also had educational potential, as Andy had to read on-screen instructions and commentaries. His parents had not shown him how to play these games, so she assumed that he had worked it out from these instructions. Indeed, as Andy initially found it difficult to settle in at school, she tried to motivate him by pointing out that learning to read would help him play new games.

Andy's parents were aware that they would soon have to start introducing rules about the amount of time he spent watching television and playing computer games because they felt there was a risk that he might spend too much time on these, to the detriment of his homework and other activities. Mrs Kerr was also uneasy about his growing interest in Game Boys and PlayStations, to which his older cousins had introduced him, as she thought he was still too young for these kinds of games.

Mrs Kerr was unsure whether the technological skills that Andy had developed at home would be of use to him at school. She did not think that the school expected children to have developed such skills before starting in P1 at four or five years old – there had never been any discussion about this. It was more important that children knew colours and numbers and could write their names. She felt that children who had not had the opportunity to develop these skills at home would be able to catch up quite quickly, and that the school would make sure that everyone was able to use the technology there.

This is where we leave these children and the others we met in the course of our research. The year or so in which we were visiting them in their families and preschools was a time of great change. Over the course of our visits there were birthdays and Christmas, some children saw the arrival of siblings and some children moved house. Families also made new acquisitions (e.g. a computer, mobile phone or video camera), and some signed up for broadband or satellite television services.

Technology could provide opportunities for learning, for fun, for communication and for self-expression; how children used it changed over time as they became more skilled, more familiar with the things they already had and what they could already do or inspired by new possibilities. Once at school, there was less time available for play at home. As they become more independent in their play and as their skills at reading, writing and drawing emerge, they might become more engaged with technology, or less so.

Children were growing up: they were getting taller, more adept and less shy. The transition to school meant new places, different friends, exposure to a diverse range of activities and less time at home. Parents wanted to prepare their children for the world of school and work, but they still wanted their children to enjoy their childhood. Although these children were growing up in a digital world, it was clear that technology was one feature among many in their lives.

The research projects

Summaries of the research projects to which we refer throughout this book are presented here. We include details of the numbers of participants, the location of the projects and the methods used to collect and analyse data. Further information is available from the project websites or associated publications. It should be noted that these studies did not focus on children with special needs, children whose main language is not English or children older than five. Definitions relating to preschool education are provided as the names given to different types of provision vary considerably across different countries. We also provide a discussion of how we thought about the ethical aspects of these studies. This should be read in conjunction with Appendix 3 as it discusses research with young children in more detail.

Ethics

There were a number of aspects of this study that required special consideration: the meaning of informed consent for young children, the use of video and photographic images of children and the conduct of fieldwork in homes. We were alert to the potential for ethical problems throughout the research, seeking advice from our advisory groups as needed. Our aim was to be respectful in our relationships with practitioners, parents and children, recognizing individual sensitivities and circumstances, and to consider the implications of our procedures during the design, execution and dissemination of the studies. All researchers were subject to vetting by Disclosure Scotland. Pseudonyms have been used throughout this book. In Appendix 3 we discuss the aspects of ethics and research methods that relate directly to participation by children.

Homes

As some of these studies involved repeated visits to families in their own homes, gaining the confidence of parents and young children and ensuring that the research was conducted ethically were key concerns. Parents received written information on the purposes of the study, the methods we were planning to use and how we intended to disseminate our findings. We considered all consent to be provisional and dependent on the evolving relationship between the families and the research team; initial written consent to participate was followed by assurances that they could withdraw at any point and further written agreement was sought on each visit. As it was possible that parents might feel obliged to continue their involvement, we offered them opportunities to withdraw during our telephone contacts and through the use of a postcard which they could return to the research team.

Typically, the first couple of visits to family homes were an opportunity for the children to get used to our presence, and we did not involve them directly in data collection. We sought the verbal consent of each child on every visit, but we went beyond this by paying careful attention to any verbal or nonverbal signs of inhibition, reluctance or discomfort as our visit proceeded. While we cannot be sure that our respondents (particularly those as young as three years old) shared our perspective on research, their continued cooperation and commitment over a series of visits suggested that they found their participation a satisfactory experience.

We also had to consider questions about the transparency of data collection (i.e. using information from our visits that had not been explicitly collected through interviews or photographs), the provision of incentives for families to participate and the implications of perceived power differentials between parents and children and the researchers. One further area of ethical concern is the impact of research in family homes on the researchers themselves. We have established a practice of paired visiting when collecting data in respondents' homes, with the co-directors responsible for debriefing members of the team after data collection, either individually or at our regular team meetings.

Nurseries

Although we were careful to consider the ethical implications of our work in nurseries, the issues were not as complex as they were when visiting family homes, and our procedures for ascertaining consents were more straightforward. However, the permissions for photographs and video recordings were given on the basis that they could be used for 'educational purposes'. This was adequate for sharing data with practitioners in different nurseries, but is more ambiguous in other contexts. The comic strip sequences are based on video recordings made in the nurseries. Individual pictures have been selected to ensure that children cannot be readily identified.

Preschool education in Scotland

The terms 'nursery' and 'playgroup' are used as follows:

> Nursery: This category includes daycare and preschool centres for children aged five or under including local authority preschool classes and nurseries; private and voluntary daycare nurseries including centres providing preschool education in partnership with the local authority; and community and workplace nurseries. The services will normally be used by parents on a regular rather than a drop-in basis and be provided at least during the school term.
>
> Playgroup: A playgroup provides sessional or day care for children aged five or under. Most are run by groups of parents with parent-led committees, although some may be owned by individuals or organised by other voluntary bodies or by the local authority. They rely heavily on parents/carers who volunteer their services although they may employ paid staff such as a play leader or assistant.
>
> (Scottish Government 2008b)

The indoor area in which children play and engage in learning activities in the nursery is known as the 'playroom'.

Summaries of the research projects

Young children learning with toys and technology at home

This project is in progress as we write this book. Funded by the Economic and Social Research Council (ESRC, RES-062–23–0507), its focus is on play at home, particularly with technological and traditional toys. This project is managed by Lydia Plowman in conjunction with Christine Stephen and Joanna McPake; the researchers who work with us are Olivia Stevenson and Claire Adey. Some of the emergent findings have informed the discussion here but most of the content of *Growing Up with Technology* is based on the following projects.

Entering e-Society: Young children's development of e-literacy

This project finished in spring 2007 and was also funded by the ESRC (RES-341–25–0034). The project investigated parents' expectations and aspirations for their children's futures as users of technology, provided observations of children using technology at home and considered the extent to which a digital divide is emerging between young children who have opportunities to make use of digital connectivity and those who do not. The project included consultation with a range of education professionals on the implications of the project's findings for early years education.

Survey

The survey and home-based case studies were conducted in four local authorities in Scotland: two with a high level of urban deprivation and two with a more mixed distribution of urban and rural and affluent and disadvantaged families. In order to ensure that the survey reached a broad spectrum of families, we selected different types of providers, including public and private nurseries, and children's centres catering for young children in need of more sustained support. Some 800 questionnaires were distributed and 346 were returned. The survey provided basic demographic data which was used to compare more and less affluent households (income of over £20,000 per year or less than £15,000 per year), to select case-study families and to contextualize the detailed data from the case studies. Survey data were analysed using Statistical Package for the Social Sciences (SPSS) to generate frequencies and cross-tabulations of the data, focusing in particular on differences between 'disadvantaged' and 'more advantaged' families.

Case studies

Families were invited to take part in the case studies on the basis of their survey responses, and selection of the 24 families was designed to ensure a balanced distribution of gender of child, family socioeconomic status and location, as well as high and low use of technology in the household. Nineteen of these families remained involved until the end of the case-study phase, which took place over a period of about 15 months. Our selection of 24 families provided a mix of 'high technology' and 'low technology' households, variation in family composition, a range of income levels and some geographical spread. The five rounds of data collection are outlined below; they were conceived by us as an iterative process that allowed us to respond to emerging issues, such as parents' reminiscences of their own uses of technology since childhood. Multiple visits also gave us the opportunity to gain an understanding of family cultures, develop relationships of trust and track changing patterns of use and attitudes. Investigating parents' understandings, aspirations and expectations drew on responses to attitudinal questions in the survey as well as the interviews spread over multiple visits. Information about our approach to involving young children in research is included in Appendix 3.

Two researchers were involved in each family visit: one audio-recorded interviews and one took field notes. Rather than transcribe tapes in their entirety, one researcher produced an account of the visit from a synthesis of information from the recording, some verbatim sequences and the field notes, and this was checked for accuracy by the other researcher.

Facilitated by NVivo, a software package for analysing qualitative data, our analyses were subject to detailed case-by-case readings of the data. The cases were representative in the sense that they highlighted some of the complexities of children's experiences with technology at home, but the particular configurations of socioeconomic status, availability of different types of technology and participants' attitudes and experiences were unique. Nevertheless, evidence from our case studies was contextualized by the survey data, and we were able to check our emergent findings over several rounds of data collection.

Expert forum

In order to gauge the relevance of our findings to current practice in preschool and primary education, we invited experts from across the UK to participate in a forum. At this forum we presented emerging findings and sought responses. This produced additional data which played a role in triangulating our earlier analyses.

Outline of data collection for Entering e-Society

The sequence of key data collection activities is summarized below.

- *Survey*: demographic information; home technology audit (resources and use); attitudes to technology and children's use.
- *Case-study families – round one*: further demographic information; more detailed technology audit; family usage of technology.
- *Case-study families – round two*: parents' educational background and experience of technology at school, work and home; child's experience of ICT at nursery; attitudes to technology use and expectations for the future.
- *Case-study families – round three*: discussion with parent and child about the technologies used by child, focusing on photographs taken by the families; further discussion about these technologies and how children learnt to use them; child demonstration of how they use a chosen item of technology.
- *Case-study families – round four*: discussion about child's non-technological activities; preparation for transition to school; involvement of child in mapping the location of technologies in the home.
- *Case-study families – round five*: update on newly acquired technologies or changes in patterns of use; family rules for use of technology; experience of transition to school, where appropriate, and use of ICT at school; activities to articulate child's perspective on preferred technologies, technologies they felt they were good at and learning how to use technolgies.

This project was managed by Joanna McPake in conjunction with Christine Stephen and Lydia Plowman; the researchers who worked with us were

Konstantina Martzoukou and Sarah Berch-Heyman. Further information is available at www.ioe.stir.ac.uk/research/projects/esociety/

Interplay: play, learning and ICT in preschool education

This project, completed in 2005, was funded by the ESRC's Teaching and Learning Research Programme (RES-139–25–0006) and investigated the ways in which children's learning with technology can be supported and enhanced in preschool settings.

The study was based in eight preschool settings. These settings represented a range of types of provision and served 400 families with a broad range of socioeconomic status. The preschool settings were formed into two cluster groups based on location. The research was undertaken in collaboration with two practitioners from each setting, at least one of whom had little or no previous experience with technologies in the playroom.

Researchers visited each of the preschool settings on seven occasions and produced baseline information, a technology audit, field notes, focused observations and video recordings. Over the course of the school year, each cluster group met with researchers four times to share observations based on video recordings and to identify ways in which practitioners could provide guided interaction and support to children using ICT within the playroom setting. During this period, each site identified two small-scale projects for implementation and evaluation that would either address recognized problems or explore new activities.

We interviewed the participating practitioners individually before and after the interventions and a questionnaire on competence and attitudes was distributed to all 40 practitioners in these settings, asking them about their perceived level of ICT competency before and after the process of guided enquiry. Conversations with children about their use of ICT in the playroom were recorded on an opportunistic basis. The video recording of playroom use of ICT was supplemented with two types of structured observations: (i) scans at regular intervals of the use of all ICTs available in the playroom and (ii) observations of target children during the nursery session.

A total of 16 hours of video data was recorded in the eight nurseries. Video recordings made during the first phase of the research were analysed in terms of interaction episodes and coded using broad categories: type of technology or other object, absence or presence of adult, the activity and the nature of the child's response. These interaction episodes were used as a way of managing the data by interpreting the start and finish of specific periods of activity with a particular object. They could be as little as 30 seconds, although five to ten minutes was typical, and could involve an individual child, a fluctuating group of children, some adult–child interaction or a combination of these. This process led to the identification of episodes in which practitioners provided support as well as examples where an absence of support led to less productive experiences for children, such as being bored or giving up an activity easily. These sequences were edited and presented to the two cluster groups as a series of video vignettes designed to stimulate reflection on their naturally occurring practice. We had identified 'guided interaction' as a potentially useful term in an earlier study in preschools (Plowman and Stephen 2005), and introduced it to practitioners in this study as a way of conceptualizing different forms of support, although we had not described its characteristics in detail at that stage. The definition of guided interaction thus developed iteratively as a result of our own analysis, combined with the practitioners' experiences and observations, and meant that findings were rooted in the culture of the playroom.

Using interaction as the unit of analysis also meant that we were using the same evidence as practitioners to interpret children's learning and behaviour. The key difference is that, as researchers, we were able to reflect on the process of interaction after the event, whereas practitioners have to make interpretive decisions in the moment. The use of video clips in the process of guided enquiry (see Appendix 2) empowered practitioners to engage in this process of analysis and reflection and share their insights. Our analysis, in turn, enabled practitioners to see their role in mediating children's interactions with ICT in a new light and to think about ways in which practice could be developed to enhance children's learning. More information on our video analysis is provided in Plowman and Stephen (2008).

Details of participating nurseries

Nursery Class A is a local authority nursery class offering part-time sessional preschool education (for three- to five-year-olds) during term time. It is situated in a primary school that serves a prosperous area with an unemployment rate below the national and local averages.

Nursery B and Out of School Care offer sessional preschool education for children aged three to five years, as well as caring for children from birth to three and some three- to five-year olds beyond their sessional hours. The centre is open from 8 a.m. to 6 p.m. for 51 weeks each year. It serves an area of high unemployment with over a third of the houses in the lowest council tax band. Children make up a quarter of the population of this former mining village.

Nursery School C is a local authority nursery school for children aged three to five years. Most children attend for preschool education sessions only, but a limited number of children stay for all or most of the day. There is provision for some children to arrive before and leave up to one hour later than the sessional hours. The area has a mix of local authority and private housing and an unemployment rate equivalent to the national average.

Nursery D is a private nursery offering care and education for children from birth to five years old. It is open for extended hours throughout the year, but children may attend for preschool education sessions only. The nursery is located in a rural area between two towns but near to a major motorway junction, giving access to popular commuter routes.

Nursery Class E is located in the shared grounds of two primary schools, one of which is denominational. It offers sessional preschool education for three- to five-year-olds during term time. It is located in an isolated village with an unemployment rate above the national and local averages and over half of the houses fall into the lowest council tax band.

Nursery Class F is part of a newly constructed primary school. Children attend for part-time preschool education sessions during term time only. It is situated in a relatively affluent area with an unemployment rate below the national and local averages and the majority of houses fall into the mid-range of council tax bands.

Nursery Class G is situated in a primary school and alongside wrap-around care provision. The nursery class offers part-time sessional preschool education during term time, but about half of the children attending use the wrap-around service before or after their time in the playroom. The area around the nursery class has very low levels of unemployment and the proportion of houses in the lowest council tax band is well below the local authority average.

Early Years Centre H offers part-time, sessional preschool education and a wrap-around service for children aged three to five. The centre is open for extended hours throughout the year. It is situated in a relatively deprived area with unemployment rates above the local and national averages. Almost one-quarter of the housing falls into the lowest council tax band and the proportion of children in the area is above the national average.

This project was managed by Lydia Plowman and Christine Stephen; the researchers who worked with us were Daniela Sime and Susi Downey. Further information is available at www.ioe.stir.ac.uk/research/projects/interplay/

Already at a disadvantage? Children's access to ICT at home and their preparation for primary school

This small-scale project was conducted during 2003–2004 and funded by the British Educational Communications Technology Association (Becta). It ran in parallel with the Interplay project and provided case studies of 16 children from nurseries involved in that project. This enabled us to look at their experiences at home and in preschool. It also featured interviews with primary school teachers about their perceptions of children's experiences of technology at home and preschool, and how these influence formal provision.

A survey produced 204 responses from parents at eight preschools – a 50 per cent response rate. The focus of the survey was on demographic information and an audit of home technologies, but we have not referred to this data in this book as it dates from 2003. This was followed by two rounds of visits to the 16 case-study families in which data was collected on demographic information, technologies in the home, children's uses of technology and their developing competences. Eight of these families were defined as 'disadvantaged' and eight as 'more advantaged'. Interviews with primary school teachers from four schools touched on their expectations of children's ICT competences as they enter school, their knowledge of children's ICT experiences at nursery and at home and their expectations of children's learning with ICT in the course of their first year of primary school (at the age of four or five).

This project was managed by Joanna McPake in conjunction with Christine Stephen and Lydia Plowman; the researcher who worked with us was Daniela Sime. Further information is available at www.ioe.stir.ac.uk/research/projects/interplay/summary.php#Disadvantage

Come back in two years! A study of the use of ICT in preschool settings

During the period 2002–2003, the Scottish government and Learning and Teaching Scotland commissioned some studies to inform the development of new policy in the area of ICT in preschool settings. This began with a review of available literature in this area (Stephen and Plowman 2003b; Plowman and Stephen 2003), and was followed by a small-scale observational study of seven preschool settings and analysis of responses to a national consultation process. Of the seven case study settings, three were local authority nursery schools, two were private sector nurseries and two were voluntary sector playgroups. They were located across several local authorities in central Scotland, in a mix of urban and rural settings. Data collection consisted of interviews with practitioners and managers, observations during two half-day sessions at each site and brief conversations with children. The observation record noted the nature and duration of each episode with ICT, the involvement of adults or other children and the level of children's engagement. The observation record also included the number of adults and children present in the setting and the ways in which practitioners were deployed. The final phase brought together the conclusions from the earlier phases and their implications for the development of a national strategy with an analysis of the responses to the consultation exercise. Responses to the consultation document came from a wide range of perspectives, including those of directors of education, early years managers and advisors, other professionals, umbrella groups, those responsible for training practitioners and interested individuals. The need for training or professional development dominated the responses, and there were concerns about equitable access to hardware and software resources across providers in the public, private and voluntary sector and ways of engaging with parents through and about ICT. This study provides a backdrop to the research described in this book but we do not make direct reference to this data.

This project was managed by Christine Stephen and Lydia Plowman.

Guided enquiry

During the research project entitled 'Interplay: Play, learning and ICT in preschool education', we investigated the nature of the guided interaction necessary to enhance children's encounters with ICT in authentic playroom contexts through a process we refer to as 'guided enquiry'. If our findings were to be useful for practitioners and make a difference to children's experiences, we had to ensure that we were studying learning in context, reflecting the everyday experiences of young children and practitioners and gathering contextualized and contingent evidence. We were keen to ensure that our research evidence was rooted in the realities of busy preschool playrooms, where the culture of practice favours play as the dominant medium for learning and children exercise choice about what to do and with whom to do it. Practitioners have to balance the sometimes conflicting demands that arise from responsibility for a range of activities happening simultaneously, as well as attend to the children's social, emotional and cognitive needs.

Guided enquiry provided an opportunity to build on practitioners' existing understanding of the playroom context and their pedagogical knowledge and experience. At a more pragmatic level, involving practitioners in the research process offered the advantage of generating data about their perceptions and experiences that would not otherwise be available and extended the duration and number of people involved in data collection. The latter is a particular advantage when, as in this case, the events under study (i.e. adults supporting children's engagement in ICT activities) could not be predicted and could be infrequent.

The practitioners from eight preschool settings, serving about 400 children, met with the researchers in two geographically-determined cluster groups four times over a period of a year or so. Following an introductory meeting of each cluster, the research team observed and video recorded playroom activity over a period of a few months, and these observations were discussed in the second meeting. On these occasions, the researchers used the video-recorded examples of children's encounters with technology as a stimulus for discussion, contributed emerging findings, helped to articulate implicit aspects of practice and supported critical reflection. The practitioners identified difficulties that they experienced with ICT, commented on the ideas presented by the researchers and on the video clips, shared practice, compared resources and planned interventions to be carried out in their own setting.

The interventions

The practitioners were invited to plan two interventions; these were small-scale projects for implementation and evaluation that would either address recognized problems integrating ICT into teaching and learning or enable the exploration of new activities or pedagogical actions. Practitioners were asked to plan at least one intervention that featured some form of ICT other than computers. Interventions involving non-computer technology included reassessing the use of the listening centre, supporting the use of digital video or still cameras in the playroom and developing children's independent use of ICT resources in the music area. Editing digital photographs, using a microscope attached to a desktop computer and exploring the use of a drawing package were among the computer-based interventions.

The practitioners' projects were discussed in the third cluster group meeting, and another project was identified at this point, initiating another cycle. A final review was held in the fourth meeting. Practitioners collected evidence during the period when they put their interventions into action, and this data was brought to the next cluster meeting. The discussions between practitioners at the cluster meeting were recorded and were a further source of evidence about the nature of guided interaction.

Collecting data

As they put their interventions into action, practitioners collected evidence to bring to the next cluster meeting. They were asked to record their experience of the process they initiated and provide evidence of the impact that the change of practice or new use of resources had on playroom activities and the children who engaged with the technology. In order to ensure authenticity, minimize the additional workload and maximize the data collected, they were invited to gather evidence in whatever forms were usual practice in their setting. As a result, the evidence that practitioners offered consisted of notes of playroom observations, photographs and extracts from children's profiles. In addition, they provided evidence from their playroom planning and review records and informal accounts of their own actions and responses to the intervention.

The research team visited each nursery seven times to collect evidence directly. We interviewed the participating practitioners individually about how they conceptualized their practice in the playroom before and after the interventions. We also surveyed all playroom staff (80 practitioners) in the participating nurseries about their self-perceived level of competency with, and attitudes to, ICT before and after the process of guided enquiry. Conversations with children about their use of technologies in the playroom were recorded on an opportunistic basis. The researchers supplemented their extensive video recording of playroom use of ICT (16 hours across the participating nurseries) with two types of structured observations: (i) scans at regular intervals of the use of all ICTs available in the playroom and (ii) observations of target children across the nursery session.

Our understanding of the nature of guided interaction evolved over the course of the project as we reviewed the video recordings and structured observations, analysed the initial interviews with practitioners and listened to the recordings of the cluster meeting discussions. Our emerging understanding was presented to practitioners during the cluster meetings, where it was endorsed, challenged or subjected to amendment. The research outcomes were therefore the result of concurrent and summative analysis of the evidence recorded by researchers and practitioners.

Appendix 3

Conducting research with young children

All of the research projects outlined in Appendix 1 involved research with children, either in their homes or at their nurseries and playgroups. We focus here on conducting research in family homes, as in Entering e-Society and Already at a Disadvantage? A fuller account, including illustrations of some of these methods, is provided in Stephen, McPake, Plowman and Berch-Heyman (2008).

In situations where children are not very vocal with visiting researchers, an over-reliance on observational methods can privilege the researcher's interpretation of events rather than the child's interpretation. Many of the standard data collection techniques used to elicit information from older children and adults, such as interviews and questionnaires, are clearly unsuitable for children of this age. In an attempt to counteract this bias, we used a variety of methods which gave prominence to the children's point of view and enabled us to consider aspects of their experience that may have been overlooked, either by us or by their parents. Given appropriate opportunities, children have valuable perspectives on their experiences, so we devised activities which were intended to appeal to them, made it easier for them to articulate what they had to say, had face validity for the children and their parents and were within the children's existing behavioural repertoires.

Although the children were often present during our interviews with their parents in rounds one and two of Entering e-Society, we did not involve them directly until the third round. (See the outline of data collection in Appendix 1.) This was conducted about six to eight months after we first met them, when they were more comfortable with the researchers being present in their homes. We had given each family an instant picture camera on our second visit with the request that they take some photographs of their child playing with technology. Our first direct conversations with the children were discussions of these photographs during our third visit, although all the children had varying degrees of involvement in our earlier interviews with their parents. In this case, most parents sat nearby while the children talked about the photographs, commenting on or elaborating on the child's response. These conversations were recorded and we always made a point of demonstrating how the technology we were using for data collection purposes worked: children were invited to turn the audio recorders on and off and could listen to themselves speaking, and a similar approach was used with the video recorders. At an appropriate point in our conversation about the photographs, we asked the child to show us how they used an item of technology, encouraging them to choose what to demonstrate. Investigating children's operational competences in this way drew on children's self-report, our own observations, parental accounts and the videos of episodes of use.

The focus of our interactions with the children in round four was a mapping exercise that was designed to explore where children used the technologies in the home and under what circumstances. We were interested in the extent to which they shared the use of some technologies with other family members, the opportunities this gave for exposure to parents or siblings modelling their use, which items were considered their own and where they were located. The children were invited to use stickers we had created in advance to represent items of furniture and technology that we knew they had to create maps of rooms in their homes. With assistance from the researcher, the child selected appropriate pictures and placed them on one sheet of paper per room. As with the photographs in round three, we recorded the conversation around this activity, as well as the visual images produced.

By round five we had been visiting the children for over one year so they now recognized at least one member of the research team who had attended every interview with each family in that period. We capitalized on this familiarity and the researcher's ability to establish a comfortable relationship with each child for the final data collection activities. The children were invited to take part in three tasks in this round: using stickers from a given range to indicate which activities they felt that they were good at; discussing how easy or difficult it would be for another child the same age to learn how to use some technologies; and sorting a range of technological and non-technological activities into those which made them happy and those which did not make them happy. Again, we used our prior knowledge of items in the house to ensure the children recognized the images we presented to them.

Ethical considerations

We focus here on the aspects of ethics that relate directly to participation by children. In Appendix 1 we outline some of our other considerations when visiting families, central to which was the paramount importance of ensuring that both parents and children were comfortable with the presence of the researchers in their homes. We used two approaches for gaining consent to participate from children.

The first approach was verbal. We asked the children if they were happy for us to talk to their parents about them and how they used technology. However,

given the imbalance in power between adults and children in these circumstances and the pressure of social conventions that are apparent to children, even
at the age of three or four, the opportunities to refuse consent are questionable.
Their agreement at this stage was therefore treated as assent (i.e. an expression
of agreement) rather than consent (i.e. explicit permission).

The second approach was behavioural, expressed through the child's
willingness to get involved with the tasks we introduced and engage in
conversations with us. Interpretation of their behaviour was usually more
straightforward: children were able to demonstrate their lack of eagerness to be
involved as they had few inhibitions about failing to respond or to complete the
tasks if they were dissatisfied or unhappy with the experience. In practice, all the
children participated in the activities introduced by the researcher in rounds
four and five with enthusiasm, although one of the activities in the final round
was shortened for those who appeared to be losing interest.

Parents were offered assurances of anonymity and confidentiality that
included secure storage of all data. At the beginning of each visit we sought
written consent from parents for each element of data collection (e.g. audio
recording, video recording and talking to children) on that day. Explicit
agreement was sought to use still and video images in a range of specified
dissemination activities, and we have been careful to respect the decision of
one family to refuse permission to use video images from their home in any
way other than for analysis internally by the team.

Bibliography

Abbs, P. and others (2006) 'Modern life leads to more depression among children', letter to the *Daily Telegraph*, 12 September 2006. Online. Available: <www. telegraph.co.uk/news/1528639/Modern-life-leads-to-more-depression-among-children.html> (accessed 6 April 2009).

Ackerman, D. and Barnett W. S. (2005) *Prepared for Kindergarten: What does 'readiness' mean?* New Brunswick, NJ: National Institute for Early Education Research.

Adams, M. J. (1990) *Beginning to read: Thinking about learning and print*, Cambridge, MA: MIT Press.

Alexander, R. (2000) *Culture and Pedagogy*, Oxford: Blackwell.

Alexander, R. (2004) 'Still no pedagogy? Principle, pragmatism and compliance in primary education', *Cambridge Journal of Education*, 34, 1: 7–33.

Alexander, R. (2006) *Towards Dialogic Teaching*, 3rd ed. Thirsk: Dialogos.

Alliance for Childhood (2004) *Tech Tonic: Towards a new literacy of technology*, College Park, MD: Alliance for Childhood.

American Academy of Pediatrics Committee on Public Education (1999) 'Media education', *Pediatrics*, 104, 2: 341–343.

American Academy of Pediatrics Committee on Public Education (2001) 'Media violence', *Pediatrics*, 108, 5: 1222–1226.

Anand, S. and Krosnick, J. (2005) 'Demographic predictors of media use among infants, toddlers, and preschoolers', *American Behavioral Scientist*, 48, 5: 539–561.

Anderson, D. and Hanson, K. (2009) 'Children, media, and methodology', *American Behavioral Scientist*, 52, 8: 1204–1219.

Antle, A. (2009) 'Embodied child computer interaction: why embodiment matters', *Interactions*, March/April, 27–30.

Aubrey, C., Bottle, G. and Godfrey, R. (2003) 'Early mathematics in the home and out-of-home contexts', *International Journal of Early Years Education*, 11, 2: 91–103.

BBC (2009) BBC Sport, Fun and games: Denise Lewis heptathlon. Online. Available: <http://news.bbc.co.uk/sol/shared/spl/hi/fun_and_games/games/heptathlon/heptathlon.stm> (accessed 16 June 2009).

Becta (2008) *Extending Opportunity*, final report of the Minister's taskforce on home access to technology, Coventry: Becta.

BERA-SIG (2003) *Early Years Research: Pedagogy, curriculum and adult roles, training and professionalism*, British Educational Research Association Early Years Special Interest Group. Online. Available: <www.bera.ac.uk> (accessed 30 April 2009).

BERR (Department for Business Enterprise and Regulatory Reform) and DCMS (Department for Culture, Media and Sport) (2009) *Digital Britain, The Interim Report*, Norwich: The Stationery Office.

Bertram, T. and Pascal, C. (2002) *Early Years Education: An international perspective*, London: Qualifications and Curriculum Authority.

Blakemore, S-J. and Frith, U. (2005) 'The learning brain: lessons for education', *Developmental Science*, 8, 6: 459–471.

Bodrova, E. (2008) 'Make-believe play versus academic skills: a Vygotskian approach to today's dilemma of early childhood education', *European Early Childhood Educational Research Journal* 16, 3: 357–369.

Bower, T. R. G. (1974) *Development in Infancy*, San Francisco: W. H. Freeman.

Bowman, B., Donovan, M. S. and Burns, M. S. (eds) (2000) *Eager to Learn: Educating our preschoolers*, Washington DC: National Academy Press.

Bronfenbrenner, U. (1979) *The Ecology of Human Development: Experiments by nature and design*, Cambridge, MA: Harvard University Press.

Brooker, L. (2002) *Starting School: Young children learning cultures*, Buckingham: Open University Press.

Bruner, O. and Bruner, K. (2006) *Playstation Nation: Protect your child from video game addiction*, New York: Center Street.

Bruner, J. S. (1996) *The Culture of Education*, Cambridge, MA: Harvard University Press.

Bryant, P. E. (1984) 'Piaget, teachers and psychologists', *Oxford Review of Education*, 10, 3: 251–259.

Buckingham, D. (2000) *After the Death of Childhood: Growing up in the age of electronic media*, Cambridge: Polity Press.

Buckingham, D. (2007) *Beyond Technology: Children's learning in the age of digital culture*, Cambridge: Polity Press.

Byron, T. (2008) *Safer Children in a Digital World: The report of the Byron Review*, Nottingham: Department of Children, Schools and Families.

Central Advisory Council for Education (1967) *Children and Their Primary Schools* (The Plowden report), London: HMSO.

Chowcat, I., Phillips, B., Popham, J. and Jones, I. (2008) *Harnessing Technology: Preliminary identification of trends affecting the use of technology for learning*. Online. Available: <www.becta.org.uk> (accessed 20 February 2009).

Cliff, D., O'Malley, C. and Taylor, J. (2008) *Future Issues in Socio-Technical Change for UK Education*, Bristol: Futurelab.

Commonwealth of Australia (2009) *Belonging, Being, and Becoming: an Early Years Learning Framework for Australia*. Online. Available: <www.deewr.gov.au/EarlyChildhood/OfficeOfEarlyChildhood/sqs/Pages/EarlyYearsLearningFramework.aspx> (accessed 6 March 2009).

Cordes, C. and Miller, E. (eds) (2000) *Fool's Gold: A critical look at computers in childhood*, College Park, MD: Alliance for Childhood.

Corsaro, W. A. (1997) *The Sociology of Childhood*, Thousand Oaks, CA: Pine Forge Press.

Cuban, L. (2001) *Oversold and Underused: Computers in the classroom*, Cambridge, MA: Harvard University Press.

Donaldson, M. (1978) *Children's Minds*, London: Fontana.

Dunn, L. and Kontos, S. (1997) 'What have we learned about developmentally appropriate practice?' *Young Children*, 52, 5: 4–13.

Dutton, W., Helsper, E. and Gerber, M. (2009) *The Internet in Britain: 2009*, Oxford: Oxford Internet Institute, University of Oxford.

Eagle, S., Manches, A., O'Malley, C., Plowman, L. and Sutherland, R. (2008) *From research to design: Perspectives on early years and digital technologies*, Bristol: Futurelab. Online. Available: <www.futurelab.org.uk > (accessed 12 April 2009).

Feiler, A. (2005) 'Linking home and school literacy in an inner city reception class', *Journal of Early Childhood Literacy*, 5, 2: 131–149.

Gee, J. (2003) *What Videogames Have to Teach us about Learning and Literacy*, New York: Palgrave Macmillan.

Gee, J. (2007) *Good Video Games + Good Learning*, New York: Peter Lang.

Gillen, J. and Hall, N. (2003) 'The emergence of early childhood literacy', in N. Hall, J. Larson and J. March (eds), *Handbook of Early Childhood Literacy*, London: Sage Publications.

Gonzalez, N., Moll, L. and Amanti, C. (eds) (2005) *Funds of knowledge: Theorizing practices in households, communities and classrooms*, Mahwah, NJ: Erlbaum.

Goodman, Y. (1986) 'Children coming to know literacy', in W. Teale and E. Sulzby (eds), *Emergent literacy: Writing and reading*, Norwood, NJ: Ablex.

Green, H. and Hannon C. (2007) *Their Space: Education for a digital generation*, London: Demos.

Gregory, E. (2005) 'Playful talk: the interspace between home and school discourse', *Early Years*, 25, 3: 223–236.

Gregory, E. (2001) 'Sisters and brothers as language and literacy teachers: synergy between siblings playing and working together', *Journal of Early Childhood Literacy*, 1, 3: 301–322.

Gutiérrez, K., Baquedano-Lopez, P. and Tejeda, C. (2000) 'Rethinking diversity: hybridity and hybrid language in the third space', *Mind, Culture and Activity*, 6, 4: 286–303.

Healy, J. (1998) *Failure to Connect: How computers affect our children's minds*, New York: Simon & Schuster.

Heath, S. (1983) *Ways with words. Language, life and work in communities and classrooms*, Cambridge: Cambridge University Press.

Honoré, C. (2008) *Under Pressure: Rescuing our children from the culture of hyper-parenting*, London: Orion.

Hughes, M. (1986) *Children and Number: Difficulties in learning mathematics*, Oxford: Blackwell.

Jenkins. H., Clinton, K., Purushotma, R., Robison, A. and Weigel, M. (2006) *Confronting the Challenges of Participatory Culture: Media Education for the 21st Century*, Chicago, IL: Macarthur Foundation.

Johnson, S. (2006) *Everything Bad is Good for You: Why popular culture is making us smarter*, London: Penguin.

Kalantzis, M. and Cope B. (2008) *New Learning: Elements of a science of education*, Cambridge: Cambridge University Press.

Kenner, C., Ruby, M., Jessel, J., Gregory, E. and Arju, T. (2007) 'Intergenerational learning between children and grandparents in East London', *Journal of Early Childhood Research*, 5, 3: 219–243.

Kent, N. and Facer, K. (2004) 'Different worlds? A comparison of young people's home and school ICT use', *Journal of Computer Assisted Learning*, 20, 6: 440–455.

Kerawalla, L. and Crook, C. (2002) 'Children's computer use at home and at school: context and continuity', *British Educational Research Journal*, 28, 6: 751–771.

Kirkorian, H., Wartella, E. and Anderson, D. (2008) 'Media and young children's learning', *The Future of Children*, 18, 1: 39–61.

Kwon, Y-I. (2003) 'A comparative analysis of preschool education in Korea and England', *Comparative Education*, 39, 4: 479–491.

Labbo, L. D., Sprague, L., Montero, M. K. and Font, G. (2000) 'Connecting a computer center to themes, literature and kindergarteners' literacy needs', *Reading Online*, 4,1. Online. Available: <www.readingonline.org/electronic/labbo/> (accessed 7 April 2009).

Lave, J. and Wenger, E. (1991) *Situated Learning: Legitimate peripheral participation*, Cambridge: Cambridge University Press.

Layard, R. and Dunn, J. (2009) *A Good Childhood: Searching for values in a competitive age*, London: Penguin.

Learning and Teaching Scotland (2003) *Early Learning, Forward Thinking: The Policy Framework for ICT in Early Years*, Dundee: Learning and Teaching Scotland.

Learning and Teaching Scotland (2009a) *Curriculum for Excellence: Technologies – principles and practice*. Online. Available: <www.ltscotland.org.uk> (accessed 7 May 2009).

Learning and Teaching Scotland (2009b) *Curriculum for Excellence: Technologies – experiences and outcomes*. Online. Available: <www.ltscotland.org.uk> (accessed 7 April 2009).

Learning and Teaching Scotland (2009c) *Sharing practice – ICT in the early years*. Online. Available: <www.ltscotland.org.uk/earlyyears/sharingpractice/ict/index. asp> (accessed 12 April 2009).

Lee, N. (2002) *Childhood and Society: Growing up in an age of uncertainty*, Buckingham: Open University Press.

Ljung-Djärf, A., Åberg-Bengtsson, L. and Ottosson, T. (2005) 'Ways of relating to computer use in pre-school activity', *International Journal of Early Years Education*, 13, 1: 29–31.

Long, S., Volk, D., Romero-Little, E. and Gregory, E. (2007) 'Invisible mediators of literacy: learning in multicultural communities', in Goodman, Y. and Martens, P. (eds), *Critical Issues in Early Literacy: Research and pedagogy*, London: Routledge.

Marsh, J. (2003) 'One-way traffic? Connections between literacy practices at home and in the nursery', *British Educational Research Journal*, 29 3: 369–382.

Marsh. J., Brooks, G., Hughes, J., Ritchie, L., Roberts S. and Wright K. (2005) *Digital Beginnings: Young people's use of popular culture, media and new technologies*, Sheffield: University of Sheffield.

McMullin, J., Comeau, T. and Jovic, E. (2007) 'Generational affinities and discourses of difference: a case study of highly skilled information technology workers', *British Journal of Sociology*, 58, 2: 297–316.

McPake, J., Plowman, L. and Stephen, C. (forthcoming) 'Digitally divided? An ecological investigation of young children learning to use ICT', *Early Childhood Development and Care*.

Moll, L., Amanti, C., Neff, D. and Gonzalez, N. (1992) 'Funds of knowledge for teaching: using a qualitative approach', *Theory into Practice*, 31, 2: 132–141.

Morrow, V. (2006) 'Understanding gender differences in context: implications for young children's everyday lives', *Children and Society*, 20, 2: 92–104.

National Association for the Education of Young Children (NAEYC) (2009) *Position Statement on Developmentally Appropriate Practice*, Washington DC: NAEYC.

Oakes, J. (2009) 'The effect of media on children: a methodological assessment from a social epidemiologist', *American Behavioral Scientist*, 52, 8: 1136–1151.

Office for National Statistics (2008) *Internet Access 2008: Households and individuals*. Online. Available: <www.statistics.gov.uk> (accessed 8 March 2009).

Palmer, S. (2006) *Toxic Childhood: How the modern world is damaging our children and what we can do about it*, London: Orion.

Pearson, J. (1999) *Women's Reading in Britain, 1750–1835: A dangerous recreation*, Cambridge: Cambridge University Press.

Piaget, J. (1926) *The Language and Thought of the Child*, New York: Harcourt, Brace.

Piaget, J. (1932) *The Moral Judgement of the Child*, London: Kegan Paul.

Piaget, J. (1954) *The Construction of Reality in the Child*, New York: Basic Books.

Piaget, J. and Inhelder, B. (1956) *The Child's Conception of Space*, London: Routledge and Kegan Paul.

Plato (2005) *Phaedrus*, trans C. Rowe, London: Penguin Classics.

Plowman, L. and Stephen, C. (2003) 'A 'benign addition'? Research on ICT and pre-school children', *Journal of Computer-Assisted Learning*, 19, 2: 149–164.

Plowman, L. and Stephen, C. (2005) 'Children, play and computers in pre-school education', *British Journal of Educational Technology*, 36, 2: 145–158.

Plowman, L. and Stephen, C. (2007) 'Guided interaction in pre-school settings', *Journal of Computer Assisted Learning*, 23, 1: 14–21.

Plowman, L. and Stephen, C. (2008) 'The big picture? Video and the representation of interaction', *British Educational Research Journal*, 34, 4: 541–565.

Plowman L., McPake, J. and Stephen C. (2008) 'Just picking it up? Young children learning with technology at home', *Cambridge Journal of Education*, 38, 3: 303–319.

Plowman L., McPake, J. and Stephen, C. (in press) 'The technologisation of childhood? Young children and technologies at home', *Children and Society*.

Plowman L., Stephen, C. and McPake, J. (in press) 'Supporting young children's learning with technology at home and in preschool', *Research Papers in Education*.

Postman, N. (1982) *The Disappearance of Childhood*, New York: Vintage Books, revised ed. 1994.

Prensky, M. (2001) 'Digital natives, digital immigrants', *On the Horizon*, 9, 5: 1–6.

Prensky, M. (2006) *Don't Bother Me Mom – I'm Learning!*, St Paul, MN: Paragon House.

Rideout, V. and Hamel, E. (2006) *The Media Family: Electronic media in the lives of infants, toddlers, preschoolers and their parents*, Menlo Park, CA: Kaiser Family Foundation.

Rideout, V. (2007) *Parents, Children and Media: A Kaiser Family Foundation survey*, Menlo Park, CA: Kaiser Family Foundation.

Rogoff, B. (1990) *Apprenticeship in Thinking: Cognitive development in social context*, New York: Oxford University Press.

Rogoff, B., Mistry, J., Göncü, A. and Mosier, C. (1993) 'Guided participation in cultural activity by toddlers and caregivers', *Monographs of the Society for Research in Child Development*, 58, 8: Serial No. 236.

Rogoff, B. (2003) *The Cultural Nature of Human Development*, New York: Oxford University Press.

Schaffer, H. R. (2004) *Introducing Child Psychology*, Oxford: Blackwell Publishing.

Scottish Consultative Council on the Curriculum (SCCC) (1999) *A Curriculum Framework for Children 3 to 5*, Dundee: Scottish Consultative Council on the Curriculum.

Scottish Executive (2007) A *Curriculum for Excellence, Building the Curriculum 2: Active learning in the early years*. Edinburgh: Scottish Executive.

Scottish Government (2008a) *The Early Years Framework*, Edinburgh: Scottish Government.

Scottish Government (2008b) *Pre-school and Childcare Statistics 2008*. Online. Available: <www.scotland.gov.uk/Publications/2008/09/12150803/0> (accessed 6 April 2009).

Shaffer, D. (2007) *How Computer Games Help Children Learn*, New York: Palgrave Macmillan.

Shaffer, D., Squire, K., Halverson, R. and Gee, J. (2005) 'Video games and the future of learning', *Phi Delta Kappan*, 87, 2: 105–111.

Shore, R. (2008) *The Power of Pow! Wham! Children, digital media and our nation's future*, New York: The Joan Ganz Cooney Center at Sesame Workshop.

Sigman, A. (2007) *Remotely Controlled: How television is damaging our lives*, London: Vermilion.

Siraj-Blatchford, I. (1999) 'Early childhood pedagogy: practice, principles and research', in P. Mortimore (ed.) *Understanding Pedagogy and its Impact on Learning* (20–45), London: Paul Chapman.

Siraj-Blatchford, I. and Sylva, K. (2004) 'Researching pedagogy in English pre-schools', *British Educational Research Journal*, 30, 5: 713–730.

Stephen, C. (2003) 'What makes all-day provision satisfactory for 3- and 4-year-olds?' *Early Child Development and Care*, 173, 6: 577–588.

Stephen, C. (2006) *Early Years Education: Perspectives from a review of the international literature*, Edinburgh: Scottish Executive Education Department.

Stephen, C. and Brown, S. (2004) 'The culture of practice in pre-school provision: outsider and insider perspectives', *Research Papers in Education*, 19, 3: 323–344.

Stephen, C. and Plowman, L. (2002) *ICT in Pre-School: A 'Benign Addition'? A review of the literature on ICT in pre-school settings*, Dundee: Learning & Teaching Scotland.

Stephen, C. and Plowman, L. (2003a) *'Come back in two years!' A study of the use of ICT in pre-school settings*, Dundee: Learning & Teaching Scotland.

Stephen, C. and Plowman, L. (2003b) 'Information and communication technologies in pre-school settings: a review of the literature', *International Journal of Early Years Education*, 11, 3: 223–234.

Stephen, C. and Plowman, L. (2008) 'Enhancing learning with ICT in pre-school', *Early Child Development and Care*, 178, 6: 637–654.

Stephen, C., Brown, S., Cope, P. and Waterhouse, S. (1998) *Quality in Pre-school Educational Provision: Staffing and staff development*, Final Report, Stirling: University of Stirling.

Stephen, C., Cope, P., Oberski, I. and Shand, P. (2008) 'They should try to find out what the children like: exploring engagement in learning', *Scottish Education Review*, 40, 2: 17–28.

Stephen, C., McPake, J., Plowman, L. and Berch-Heyman, S. (2008) 'Learning from the children: exploring preschool children's encounters with ICT at home', *Journal of Early Childhood Research*, 6, 2: 99–117.

Stevenson, O. (2008) 'Ubiquitous presence, partial use: the everyday interaction of children and their families with ICT', *Technology, Pedagogy and Education*, 17, 2: 115–130.

Strand, T. (2006) 'The social game of early childhood education', in J. Einarsdottir and J. T. Wagner (eds) *Nordic Childhoods and Early Education* (71–99), Greenwich, CT: Information Age Publishing.

Sylva, K., Taggart, B., Siraj-Blatchford, I., Totsika, V., Ereky-Stevens, K., Gilden, R. and Bell, D. (2007) 'Curricular quality and day-to-day learning activities in pre-school', *International Journal of Early Years Education*, 15, 1: 49–65.

Sutton-Smith, B. (1997) *The Ambiguity of Play*, Cambridge MA: Harvard University Press.

Tapscott, D. (1998) *Growing Up Digital: The rise of the net generation*, New York: McGraw Hill.

Tharp, R. and Gallimore, R. (1989) *Rousing Minds to Life: Teaching, learning and schooling in social context*, Cambridge: Cambridge University Press.

Thomas, G. (2007) *Education and Theory: Strangers in paradigms*, Maidenhead: Open University Press.

Tizard, B. and Hughes, M. (1984) *Young Children Learning: Talking and thinking at home and at school*, London: Fontana.

Tizard, B., Mortimore, J. and Burchell, B. (1981) *Involving Parents in Nursery and Infant Schools*, London: Grant McIntyre.

Uprichard, E. (2008) 'Children as 'being and becomings': children, childhood and temporality', *Children and Society*, 22, 4: 303–313.

U.S. Department of Education (2002) *No Child Left Behind*, part D, Section 2042, 'Enhancing Education Through Technology'. Online. Available: <www.ed.gov/policy/elsec/leg/esea02/pg34.html> (accessed 5 April 2009).

Vincent, C., Ball, S. and Kemp, S. (2004) 'The social geography of childcare: making up a middle-class child', *British Journal of Sociology of Education*, 25, 2: 229–244.

Vygotsky, L. (1962) *Thought and Language*, Cambridge, MA: MIT Press.

Vygotsky, L. (1978) *Mind in Society: The development of higher psychological processes*, Cambridge, MA: Harvard University Press.

Weigel, M., James, C. and Gardner, H. (2009) 'Learning: peering backward and looking forward in the digital era', *International Journal of Learning and Media*, 1, 1: 1–18.

Wells, G. (1999) *Dialogic Inquiry: Toward a sociocultural practice and theory of education*, Cambridge: Cambridge University Press.

Welsh Assembly Government (2008) *Framework for Children's Learning for 3 to 7-year-olds in Wales*, Cardiff: Welsh Assembly.

Winn, M. (2002). *The Plug-In Drug: Television, computers and family life*, Penguin 25th anniversary edition, New York: Penguin Putnam.

Wood, D., Bruner, J. and Ross, G. (1976) 'The role of tutoring in problem solving', *Journal of Child Psychology and Psychiatry*, 17, 2: 89–100.

Yelland, N., Lee, L., O'Rourke, M. and Harrison C. (2008) *Rethinking Learning in Early Childhood Education*, Maidenhead: Open University Press.

Index